RECIPES FOR
A NEW NORMAL

OUR FOOD, OUR RIGHT: 3RD EDITION

A Community Alliance for Global Justice Publication

Papercut by Nikki McClure

Cover illustration copyright © Morgan Brown
Cover & book design by David Rollins & Alanna Peterson

Paperback ISBN: 978-1-952149-00-9

Printed and bound in the United States of America
First printing 2021

Published by CAGJ: Community Alliance for Global Justice & Rootcity Press
Seattle, Washington
cagj.org
rootcitypress.com

Community Alliance for Global Justice

is a grassroots organization in Seattle working to strengthen the global food sovereignty movement through community education and mobilization. By engaging in popular education, direct action, and anti-oppressive organizing and community building, the Food Justice Project seeks to challenge and transform the globalized, industrial, corporate-driven food system and promote existing alternatives.

Check out our website at https://cagj.org and feel free to drop us a line at contact_us@cagj.org.

To experience this zine in a digital format
with added accessibility features, visit our website:

https://zine.cagj.org

*In memory of Lillian,
who embodied that to cook is to love,
and everyone else we have lost.*

May they rest in power and peace.

We believe:

Food is life. And this pandemic year, with all its challenges, is ripe with stories about life-affirming food projects that deserve to be honored.

Documentation is valuable. Capturing the stories of survival and resilience that have marked this unprecedented year is a reminder of our ability to survive, to persist, and to dream new worlds into being.

Storytelling is a superpower. Narrative crafting and community building are tools of resistance.

Art is healing. Creating together and thinking beyond what exists now fuels us.

Culture is a tool to live out our liberation.

Food Sovereignty takes many forms. We feature that diversity to reaffirm that a food sovereign world is not only possible, and necessary if we want to survive, but beautiful too.

Table of Contents

Continued...

Photo by David Rollins

Letter from the Coordinator

Dear Reader,

While I hadn't ever co-created a zine before this one, I have planted many seeds, and I can't help but make the parallel between these acts. The process of planting seeds for me is as material as it is spiritual, whereby I make a commitment to the earth and reaffirm my belief in the radical power of hope. It is also a practice in leaning into community (human and more-than-human alike) and trusting the process. The development of this zine has been similar on all accounts.

What began as an idea over a year ago grew steadily into what appears before you thanks to many caring hands, heads, and hearts. Initially I wasn't sure how long it would take or what it would look like or whose art it would feature. All I knew is that it was needed. I craved a container for intentionally holding stories from these moments amidst historic crises; a space we could return to in order to remember, to learn, to grieve, to witness, to celebrate, and to connect—with ourselves, each other, and this world.

So as the COVID-19 pandemic worsened and we were forced to disconnect from what we loved, we invited artists to tell us about (re)connecting through food. We hoped that their stories would help us traverse through this portal into a new world more abundant with justice, beauty, and healing for all. Inside these pages, you'll find piece after piece of wisdom that we hope you can return to as needed for nourishment through the crises that may come before us yet. We titled this zine "Recipes for a New Normal" because what is a recipe but a story about how to nourish ourselves?

Coordinating this zine has been a tremendous gift and an opportunity to practice building new ways of being together. We set out with a commitment to intentionality, equity, and collaboration and these guiding principles were as present in the process as they are in the product. We paid our artists for their work, moved at a life-affirming speed, and collaborated with love. We also centered accessibility, both in terms of disability justice (by creating a digital version which includes audio recordings and alt text for each piece), and economic justice (by including sliding scale purchase options for the print version and offering honorariums with priority to BIPOC, disabled, and queer creators).

I must end with gratitude. Many thanks to all our contributors. To the Organizing Collective members. To those who donated. To those who fed us throughout. And always, to the past and present stewards of the land that nourishes us from the roots.

In loving solidarity,

Momo Wilms-Crowe (on behalf of the Organizing Collective)
Zine Coordinator and Food Justice Project Co-Chair

Zine Organizing Collective

Momo Wilms-Crowe	Sam Shafer
David Rollins	Erika Mazza-Smith
Pukhraj Sidhu	Sara Lavenhar
Nuansi	Sophia Kimble
Alanna Peterson	Connor Nakamura
Heather Day	Noël Hutton
Delia Pinto-Santini	Lynx Patrice Hawthorn

Ella's Song: We Who Believe in Freedom Cannot Rest Until It Comes

By Heather Day

Ella's Song is a freedom song. Written by Bernice Reagon and performed a cappella by the group she founded in 1973, Sweet Honey in the Rock, the song honors the activist Ella Baker. A hero of the civil rights movement, Baker played critical roles in building collective power for racial and economic justice in the southern United States. She led many successful organizing drives working with the NAACP, Southern Christian Leadership Conference, Student Nonviolent Coordinating Committee, and many other organizations, with a special appreciation for nurturing young peoples' roles in movements for human rights. Bernice Reagon is a living legend herself, whose legacy includes bringing a cappella freedom songs to the center of movement-building.

Singing is a way I connect that was disrupted by the pandemic. This disconnection meant not being able to gather anymore in person with my friends and fellow CAGJ comrades Jenny and Marina, with whom I sang Ella's Song in the recording. It has been exciting to discover new ways of making music together, without really being together. Yet all musicians yearn for in-person music making to re-become who we really are. I've felt heartsick without that collective experience, my best form of therapy.

This song has particular significance for me as it represents a legacy that has seen seismic shifts since George Floyd was murdered by Derek Chauvin one year ago to the day I write these words. The year 2020 will always be remembered as a critical turning point in consciousness raising and mobilization, thanks to the hundreds of thousands of people who took to the streets and used every possible avenue to build the Black Lives Matter movement into such a critical force for change.

It was painful to mostly witness the movement explode from home. As someone with a compromised immune system and just a year out from cancer treatment, I had too many Covid-related fears to partake in many street protests in 2020. It hurt my heart to not be there, and I was triggered watching the police brutality live-streamed late at night, my heart racing from a place that saw similar events unfold in 1999 during the WTO mobilizations. I felt rage at the police and Seattle Mayor, and awe and gratitude for everyone participating and putting their lives on the line, particularly BIPOC organizers who even experimented with what freedom looks like in the Capitol Hill Autonomous Zone, including by farming in Cal Anderson Park.

The Food Sovereignty movement is my home, and I am grateful to be part of this meaning-making that is our 3rd Zine. In this year of disconnect, CAGJ has brought powerful online connection with a worldwide community with whom I collaborate. This year has taught me to always bring song along when we gather to organize, and take to the streets! It helps create the joy we need to feel to keep fighting for freedom until we win.

Hear Ella's Song sung a capella by Heather Day, Jenny McIntosh and Marina Skumanich in the digital zine.

https://zine.cagj.org/art/heather-jenny-marina

Heather Day (she/her), **Jenny McIntosh** (she/her), and **Marina Skumanich** (she/her)

Heather, Jenny and Marina sing together whenever they can. They believe that joy and justice, music and marching, and singing and solidarity all go hand-in-hand. For their day jobs, Heather is CAGJ's Director, and a co-founder. Jenny is Operations Manager at the Tenants Union of Washington State, and Marina works to improve drought prediction and response at NOAA.

Within the backward and upside down flight of hummingbirds

a great blue heron's ballad   billows:

      what is free in this bread-and-butter   fixed order
its red-lined tape binding   legs and feet? Inside

      beguiling pistons heave tight hems: we're as free
as my cat is to leave the house.   Tell me friend,

          are we tracking something new,   honestly
I'm nothing but weary from Colorado to Lamma Island
      yet never-   the-less

have your feathers, like   a chickadee,

      become puffed armor — for generations   legs and
feet lay bare and uninsulated   meeting a blitz

      of wind and ice-covered words. I hear   some birds stay
and face the middle of that   dark winter's night

         contrary to seemingly impossible   odds.
I wish to be like a superb lyrebird with the loudest
     call in the world — I   would sing —

Who has toilet paper and   can you leave me some?

      Really, it's as absurd as a waterfall with no   fall.
In my opinion   we've come   undone but few

      move within a perennial pendulum that is   soaked
in the ancestor's tale, when   we will wake

while capitalism burns lenity and   hope
tell me friend of your skill in palm and I will share
mine — perhaps   it's grassy

to purify and calm or   the hullabaloo of teas

and tinctures, a loamy sower or a seed   saver
for when all becomes dead   of night maybe

you are a craftsman for a frosty dawn.   The song
of the morning bird drifts   me awake —

a new season is coming they cheep   and warble,
sometimes I worry that winter birds will freeze near
such cold nights   with modest

legs and feet, but they   are surprisingly well

adapted — they will not freeze below zero —   it is not
simply north in spring nor   south

in winter — migration is rooted   in our bones.
Tell me, can we greet winter like a dark-eyed junco?
with a chortle.

See Laura's recipe for Roasted Root Vegetable Soup on page 116!

Laura Titzer (she/her)

Laura lives on the native lands of the Coast Salish/Stillaguamish/
Duwamish/Muckleshoot/Suquamish where Seattle, WA resides and
is a writer, a lover of story, and constantly ablaze for learning, facili-
tation, and social change. She's previously been published in *Gastro-
nomica*, *Kosmos*, and *A Growing Culture* and is the author of *No Table
Too Small*. She writes about social change, feminism, and decentering
white dominant culture. She lives in adoration with her partner, cat,
and ferrets.

Sqəlᶜ's Garden: Indigenous Food & Medicine Sovereignty Garden

Carvers' Camp Canoe Family

* sqəlač, the Octopus
* S. Lushootseed Language.

Nuansi 2021

sqələč's garden

By Nuansi

Backstory to my drawing:
The Roots of the Garden

Since the 1980s, the Coast Salish and other Indigenous Nations have travelled as Canoe Families each summer up and down the Salish Sea on the InterTribal Canoe Journey (also called Tribal Canoe Journey), the same way their ancestors always travelled before their tradition was almost lost due to colonialism. The direction of the Journey depends on which Nation or Tribe is the year's host. The Paddle to Lummi 2019 had over 100 canoes land, and over 10,000 people joined in the Journey.

The octopus in the drawing is special because she represents the Umiak our Canoe Family journeys in. An Umiak is a type of canoe. Ours is named sqələč, the Southern Lushootseed word for octopus. (Southern Lushootseed is the language spoken mainly by Duwamish, Puyallup, Suquamish, Nisqually, Muckleshoot,

Snoqualmie and Squaxin Tribes in the general areas now called Seattle down to Olympia in Washington.) Our Umiak and most of our Canoe Family members live in this area. Our Umiak has an octopus design on her sides.

We were all looking forward to joining the InterTribal Canoe Journey last summer with sqǝlǝč. To the excitement of being out on big water in the small open Umiak. And spending about two weeks camping along the beautiful Salish Sea, ending with the week-long, formal tradition of gifts exchange, thanks and dance. Also with meeting new friends and old from other Canoe Families. But due to the pandemic, the 2020 Paddle to Snuneymuxw, to Nanaimo, British Columbia, was cancelled. Even though we were glad to protect each other and the larger community, it was so disappointing!

Canoe Journey is a very healing inner journey. When it was cancelled, a few members of our Canoe Family got together to do something different. We wanted a safe and healing way to come together again. We came together to create a food and medicine garden for one of our elders, Philip H. Red Eagle (Dakota and Salish). He is one of the important people who helped shape the Canoe Journey movement! Philip H. Red Eagle is also the person who invited me into his Canoe Family as a non-Native person. Always busy and helping others, he has never had a garden.

Friends and allies helped donate Native plants, herbs, seeds and soil. We shared a feeling of family and happiness to create something healing during the pandemic. We finished the garden beds on Indigenous Peoples' Day 2020. Happy to celebrate in such a special way.

Usually, our Canoe Family connects with the Salish Sea, but this time we connected with the land. Digging and planting together we grow roots in a different way. It is an unexpected gift to have the time and energy to focus on the land, and give back to our elder who is one of the visionaries of the Tribal Canoe Journey's Resurgence movement all those years ago.

Nuansi (she/they)

I am a recent University of Washington graduate with a dual major in American Indian Studies and Comparative History of Ideas. In 2020 my art was published in the Raven Chronicles Press's Anthology, *Take a Stand: Art Against Hate*. My intersecting identities bring awareness to stories in the margin. An invited member of a Coast Salish Canoe Family, I am a puller in our Umiak named sqələč, 'the octopus'. Indigenous Sovereignty is close to my heart. I've been deeply influenced by the sea, plants and animals of Thailand, where I grew up.

what is being fed

By Alanna Peterson

the crow appeared in our garden
one day in pandemic-spring.
cherry blossom petals dotted
the ground still: our only measure
of time passing. the crow
watched us approach through
blue-rimmed eyes
but stood motionless. too young
to be afraid. or perhaps
extremely afraid
but
unable to flee

                              how strange it is when art
                                   springs into life.
                        this crow for example, fluttering
                                   out of my pages,
                           conjured into being through
                                scribbles on paper,
                            their fate flowing out
                                   from my pen

the children made the crow a nest
out in the back corner of the garden.
what should we feed it,
they asked. sunflower seeds
were all we had.
we sprinkled them in the grass
while the crow watched. disinterested.
other crows swooped down to squawk
at the young one and i told myself
we had done what we could.
now the crows
would take care of their own

how can i claim
that this crow appeared
because of my stories?
when my stories
were never only mine.
they were borrowed things
flowing in on some mysterious current,
and i held them
barely long enough
to understand

in the end, this story
was a short one. next morning
the crow was no more. torn apart
by some predator, threadlike entrails
decorating the grass, head bleeding
on the steps of the garden shed.
sometimes even flowing water
cuts like a claw. the price of creation
is to see it mirrored in a thousand ways.
it isn't always clear
what is being fed

how often stories end here:
the blood on the pavement.
the cold eternity of the grave. but where is
the true end? or is the end never true?
the sunflower seeds nestling
into soil fed by a bird's
hollow bones.
the yellow blossoms
lifting their faces
to the sun
of a new spring.

Alanna Peterson (she/her)
Alanna loves digging in the dirt, learning languages, creating elegant
spreadsheets, and challenging systems of oppression. She is the author
of a series of young adult thrillers inspired by food justice movements.
To learn more about her work, visit alannapeterson.com/stories.

making room for the unexpected

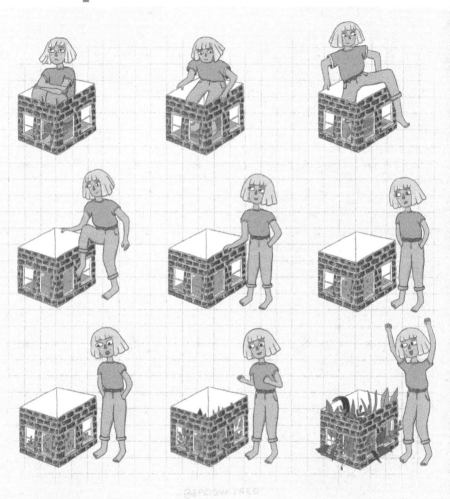

Tess Keesling (they/she)

Tess is a queer creative making plant-based art and educational material under the pseudonym Sprigwizard. Raised at a competitive dance studio in a food swamp north of Detroit, MI, Tess now resides in Seattle, WA where she is perfecting her chocolate chip cookie recipe, making comics, and learning about plants. See Tess's art animated in the digital zine.

Miracles

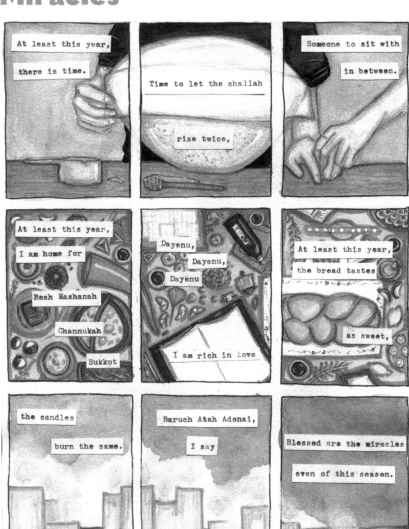

Forest Rolnick-Wihtol (they/them)

Forest is a queer & Jewish multi-media artist living in rural Oregon on occupied Kalapuya land. Find more of their art on Instagram: @ofbosque.

A Soffritto Story

By Grace Miyoshi

I hate food, is the biggest lie I could ever tell. No, never. I really just hate the costs of food. I'm a full-time student, a part-time worker, and a new "adult" with all the responsibilities that come with the title. Being fully independent for the first time in my life this year, I'm confronted with the realities of budgeting. If I'm being honest, I've managed my spreadsheets poorly. Not at all really. With the measly 24 hours we get in a day, sitting down to update my budgeting seems trivial. This avoidance, de-prioritization might just be a mask for my true fear of discovering an overarching and blatantly obvious truth: I don't have any money.

A tight timeline and an even tighter budget have elicited a number of visits to the free student food pantry for me. On top of the one allotted protein, canned item, and grain per person, the pantry offers a myriad of grocery 'freebies'. These items are supplied by supermarket donations consisting of imperfect foods and items on the verge of expiration that can no longer be sold in store. Food waste is turned to food assurance for those facing insecurity. For this reason, I am grateful for the byproduct of a perfection-driven capitalistic food culture that has mercifully filled my fridge.

Among the unpredictable variety of produce and fare I receive at the food pantry, there are always three constants: onions, carrots, and celery. This culinary combination is disguised under different aliases: mirepoix, soffritto, sofrito, suppengrün, pinçage, and I'm sure, many more. As an amateur, self-taught cook, I had no idea what mirepoix was. I did, however, know what dishes like Bolognese, Japanese mince-meat curry, mixed vegetable soup, Japanese fried-rice, and Jambalaya were. The same could be said about the millions of chefs-in-their-own-right that are out there in the world, knowing the dishes but not the name of their culinary foundation. It took a year of living away from home, hours of Pinterest scrolling, and multiple visits to the student food pantry for me to realize that the most delicious and familiar dishes are all thanks to the mirepoix. These three humble vegetables-turned-soffritto are the base of various exquisite and ethnic dishes that span all cultures and economic classes. With a multicultural background and both experiences of economic security and insecurity, the mirepoix has been subconsciously, and now consciously, a core of my life.

So, here, I wanted to impart to you my mirepoix memoir, a soffritto story.

My lower back aches from the hours at my desk on Zoom classes and ankles and knees are sore from a 6-hour shift. Nonetheless, my body is unwavered in the brace of my electric stove top. I'm overcome with exhaustion and hunger, but mostly a looming sensation of anxious nausea. Out of all the things I have to do in a day, I try not to make cooking another task. Easier said than done. But the truth is simple—tired work anxiety can't really be negotiated these days, but hunger is always curable with a home-cooked meal.

So, time to cook. I'm making my mom's Bolognese meat sauce, vegetarian version.

I peer into my fridge, the yellow light illuminating our unusually full array of foods. Methodically, I grab the large stalk of celery, some broken carrots rods, and the pack of Beyond ground meat I splurged $10 on at Trader Joe's. Taking a few steps to the pantry cupboard, I quickly grab some cans of diced tomatoes, a couple onions, and spices. I spend at least 20 minutes finely mincing first the celery, then the peeled carrots, and finally the onions. I miss my mom's food processor. Switching back and forth between standing on my left and right foot, I mindlessly pop my knees one after the other to relieve the pressure. The mincing is oddly a moment of serenity—a mundane task with no thoughts, only the sounds of the crunching vegetables to keep me company.

Food prep finished, I start sautéing the onions, and add the carrots and celery. I'm mesmerized by the glowing swirls of orange, green, and white. The pot is a pixelated abstract painting, bursting with complementary colors. Just as quickly as the art show came together, the vegetables released their cool, aromatic steam that consumes my kitchen. Although standing in my compact, dim-lit apartment, the scent instantly transports me to my parents' house. I don't feel my sore body. Rather, I feel myself moseying out of my bedroom and creaking up the stairs, the smell of food drawing me out of my comfortable room. The same warming scent of onion, carrots, and celery fill the halls. "Mmmmm, it smells good, what's for dinner?" is my usual catch phrase. Judging by the smell, the final dish could be any one of my mom's signatures: Bolognese, Japanese mince-meat curry, tomato vegetable soup, or Japanese fried rice. Any answer was a good answer. For me, soffritto invites curiosity and invokes eagerness for an unknown meal with certain satisfaction.

Before my mom can reply, my mind returns to reality. I nearly stir the bright colors to muddled caramel brown, not typically desired in mirepoix. I hurriedly place the mixture aside in a separate bowl and reheat the pot to start browning the meat. Aware of the time left in the night to complete assignments, send emails, and finish readings, I don't linger on the other steps. I know this recipe like the back of my hand, somehow picking it up naturally over the months and years of my mom making it. The ingredients have never been measured for me either; it's just a feeling. I quickly mix together the rest of the ingredients and start to let the sauce simmer.

Waiting for the sauce to thicken, I try to sit back at my desk for work. My mind drifts with the lingering soffritto aroma. My work anxiety dissipates, replaced by pride in my Bolognese recreation. I'm hungry for pasta and continue to contemplate my magic mirepoix moment that brought me back home. It was a soffritto epiphany that reminded me that the best and most diverse dishes are derived from the same three humble ingredients. Suddenly, I can imagine all the royal cooks, home-chefs, and foodies before me who must have experienced the same enveloping soffritto aroma. Alone with the inescapable smell of home, I am simultaneously surrounded by all the dishes and all the people connected to the mirepoix. Onion, celery, and carrots are ingredients not subject to change in smell, taste, or texture—they are eternal constants in our culinary world. The mirepoix connects generations, economic class, and global cultures. Now, the mirepoix connects me to the present, a singular Bolognese moment. It also connects me to my mom, my past, and all of our home meals. And it also connects me to the diverse, versatile world of historical and cultural cuisine. Mirepoix is the epitome of food's connective capacity. The taste and smell of onions, celery, and carrots mean the same thing across all languages—food is love.

Tonight, I already knew what I was making, but the scent of the soffritto is still reminiscent of endless possibility. No matter what you make out of the threesome, no matter how the recipes change, the base will always stay the same. And, proudly holding my plate of rigatoni Bolognese, I smile in the peace and power of the culinary arsenal that my mom gifted to me.

This is my mirepoix memoir, but really, the soffritto story will forever and always be ours.

I have included two recipes (see pages 120 and 122) that are very special to me. I hope the smells of soffritto remind you of something or someone, if not, then simply the joys of heartwarming food.

Grace Miyoshi (she/her)
Grace is a student at the University of Oregon, studying in the School of Journalism and Communication, and an aspiring blog writer, documenting the connective powers of food and fashion. Her first love was and is food; she will continue to spread the joys and love of food through cooking, writing, and connecting.

For an enlarged version...

Visit the digital zine:
https://zine.cagj.org/art/erika-mazza-smith/

Sourdough Futures

BUBBLING IN SOURDOUGH STARTERS ACROSS THE WORLD IS THE FUTURE

YEASTY IDEAS

WE FEED OUR SOURDOUGH FUTURE EVERYDAY, NURTURING THEM WITH FRESH FLOUR AND WATER

YES, MORE THAN HALF OF THE STARTER HAS TO BE "DISCARDED" TO CULTIVATE A HEALTHY STARTER BUT THIS DISCARD CAN BE GIVEN TO FRIENDS TO CREATE NEW STARTER OR BAKED INTO OTHER THINGS INFINITE POSSIBILITIES AND FUTURES

AFTER ALL THE PURPOSEFUL CARE, TENDING AND NURTURANCE, THE STARTER DOUBLES IN SIZE!

GOOD CONDITIONS FOR A HEALTHY FUTURE (ANCHORED IN OLD TRADITIONS)

TIME TO BUILD OUR FUTURE FIRST, MIX TOGETHER FLOUR, WATER AND SALT LET THIS SIT AND WARM UP TO THE STARTER WE GOTTA BE PATIENT! BUILDING A FUTURE IS NOT AN EASY FEAT

A FEW HOURS LATER WE ADD SOME STARTER MIX IN WELL AND LET THE DOUGH REST ENJOY THE PROCESS....

LET THE DOUGH FERMENT THE DOUGH MOVES SLOW AND AT ITS OWN PACE EVERY HOUR OR SO WE CAN STRETCH AND FOLD THE DOUGH (GENTLY!)

AFTER OUR DOUGH HAS RESTED AND RISEN, NOW IT IS TIME TO SHAPE HOW DO WE WANT OUR FUTURE TO LOOK?

WE LET THE FUTURE COOL DOWN FOR A WHILE, PREPPING IT FOR WHAT LAYS AHEAD

WHEN IT HAS COOLED WE PUT IT INTO A HOT DUTCH OVEN (THE UNIVERSE?) THE FUTURE IS BECOMING SOLIDIFIED AND REAL IT'S HAPPENING! OUR HARD WORK IS PAYING OFF!

IN ALL THESE STEPS IS ANIEXTY, FEAR AND CONFUSION.
WHAT IF THIS DOESN'T WORK?
WHAT IF THIS IS TOO HARD?
WHAT IS THAT WEIRD SMELL?
HOW DO WE FIX THIS?

IT'S OKAY!

IT CAN BE HARD TO KNOW HOW OUR SOURDOUGH WILL TURN OUT.

BUT IN THE END THERE WILL BE BREAD EVEN IF ITS NOT PERFECT, EVEN IF IT DIDN'T RISE A LOT, EVEN IF.

IF IT REALLY DOESN'T WORK, THERE WILL STILL BE STARTER AND WE CAN TRY AGAIN

IN FACT WE MUST TO KEEP A STARTER GOING YOU GOTTA KEEP FEEDING IT, MUCH LIKE A FUTURE. THE WORK NEVER REALLY ENDS WE CONTINUE BAKING

Erika Mazza-Smith (she/her)

Erika is an illustrator and comics artists living on Duwamish land (aka Seattle, WA).

To Build in Place

By David Rollins

Gardening began for me as an act of defiance. Several things sparked this: undeniable evidence that a climate crisis was already upon us, that for decades those in power knew about its looming consequences, the gravitational pull toward business as usual I saw around me, and that my ancestors—being settlers in a land they ecologically and culturally knew little of—were complicit in the process. Coming to understand all this was a shock to my system, a guttural shattering of a myth I'd been saturated in.

Learning more that agriculture, in its connection to emissions, deforestation, waterway pollution, was part and parcel of environmental degradation and historically a foundational excuse deployed for the seizing of Indigenous lands in the only state I knew by heart...very quickly the food meant to nourish me too became distasteful. All traced with hints of a destructive past that lingered in my mind after they vanished from my tastebuds, a sort of numbness took over.

Still, I felt compelled to plant something. Anything, really, if only for the increased biomass. Even if it didn't fruit, maybe it could feed a pollinator or two. So in the neglected edges of a lawn, where a deck had burned down and each trowel-full of soil brought up new items of unique and forgotten trash, it began. Watering and waiting, often staring at the plants.

Impatiently anxious for their next move, all while anticipating the next transplant because I learned that some plants collaborate, co-conspiring in mutual wellbeing, fixing nitrogen underground and warding off aphids of danger and giving shelter for insects of promise. When in communion with others, I learned these garden plants practiced the same services that some of us call "mutual aid," working to build reciprocal relationships in unlikely places. What unfolded for me was a model of living beyond the rugged individualism that I was given. In that came a lifestyle where neighbors

31

share with one another, where the network of rooted living is cultivated intentionally, one that yields promise out of sites tended from care.

Several seasons down the line, these seedlings were sown in the midst of early spring in a cold windowsill, as lockdown blanketed the Northwest. Admittedly, a cold windowsill, in a poorly insulated home atop a sinking foundation built on the old flood plain of the Willamette, may have still not been the ideal home for young sunflowers. However, in urban gardening, frequently the not-so-ideal is what we have at hand and often the very place we transform into one of renewal. The arena where we assess the damage, and calculate the strategies needed for healing. Where reconciliation lays embedded in the soil, also buried in waiting: offering a practice grounds for the community we wish to breathe into being.

At summer's end, many seedlings even thrived, growing taller than any human neighbor who walked by or friend who found (distanced) refuge in the lawn-turned-garden that sat beneath the flowers. Who, each positioned best toward the sun, oversaw neighborhood concerts, sunset skates, bike rides, everyday zooms, and the growing threads of community interconnection born from passing encounters. Through a sense of resistance emerged exactly those grounds to work through the unknowing, the uncertainty that permeated all of 2020. Ultimately, somewhere to weather, to dream, to build in place.

David Rollins (he/him)

David is a photographer, occasional writer, and urban farmer currently living in Tohono O'odham and Pascua Yaqui lands. As a recent graduate from the University of Oregon, he studied the intersections of anthropology, environmental studies, and civic agriculture. When not gardening, David is an avid cyclist, reader, and forager.

In urban gardening, frequently the not-so-ideal is what we have at hand and often the very place we transform into one of renewal.

—DAVID ROLLINS

Roots

somewhere between
her mother's ocean eyes
& her father's leather hands,
she searches for land that will take her

she defines the places she goes
by their shades of green
& she envies them all
for their roots

she wonders if her love affair with growing
is a symptom of displacement

she pleas to the soil –
if i learn you well enough,
will you hold me as your own?

and when she buries her hand,
lifts & listens,
the soil responds –
watch the squash leaves unfurl,
see how their veins river the same as yours.
you have always been me,
& i have always been you.

aubrey pongluelert (she/her)
aubrey is an Asian-American artist, food grower, and community
organizer based in Missoula, MT (Selis and Ktunaxa lands), where
she recently received her MS in Environmental Studies: Sustainable
Food and Farming. aubrey's passion and work centers around the
interconnections between food justice, creative eco-storytelling,
and intersectional ecofeminism. She finds delight in running fingers
through bags of seeds, embroidering while listening to Joni Mitchell,
and jumping into alpine lakes.

Huerto de la Familia

The woman in the foreground with the hat was who I had the pleasure of helping. I wish I could recall her name as I think of her sometimes.

Our communication was limited in that her English was limited and my Spanish was just sad. But we could exchange pleasantries: hello, how are you, I'm fine how are you, good thank you. But after that it was lots of sí's and no's. I worked with nimble fingers untangling the tendrils from each other, or at least that's what I gathered as she mimed my hands rapidly with a large grin on her face. She excitedly reached into the vines and picked a small but still very green, and very unscathed bean. She offered it to me, I accepted. I was unsure if she was bragging about her crop or if she wanted me to eat it, perhaps both.

I mustered the little Spanish I knew from TV: "C-comida..?"

Her eyes widened and she did a little shuffle in the mangled vines. "Sí!! Comida!!"

We couldn't discuss much, but we were both equally as excited over our shared understanding of this little green bean.

This experience holds even more meaning to me because of the importance Momo had placed on seed sovereignty before our visit to the farm. I had never considered the threat to biodiversity and community independence that big seed companies posed. So taking all the dead soybean plants which looked sad and wasted, picking these small dry husks from them, and pulling out these soft still alive seeds, felt very different than the emotionless trip to a hardware store where one would pick a glossy plastic package filled with seeds that were dead but somehow produced life. The hardware store seeds feel empty. The soybeans had potential.

Evelyn Costello (she/they)
I'm a 20 year old lesbian artist based in Eugene, OR, who just wishes to have a cottage and live off the land. I do ceramics and photography, primarily with a focus in visual anthropology. I love food and learning about the cultures and traditions behind different cuisines. I would consider cooking one of my love languages, and as my dad always told me, "If you love someone, cook them good food."

38

Adopt a Seed: Seed Heritage of the People for the Good of Humanity

By Tyler Short

This is a short story about my role as a guardian of R3R—Rhodelia Triple Rainbow—the beloved dent corn grown collectively by Sustainable Agriculture of Louisville (SAL) and individually by our members and friends.

Here in the Ohio River Valley, the land that we work was, prior to colonization, a crossroads for multiple indigenous tribes, including the Shawnee, Creek, Cherokee, and Great Lakes peoples. While honoring their many contributions to humanity, we lament the injustices that initiated settler colonialism and examine our complicity in its continuation. Historical memory and collective action are truly necessary to achieve a Just Transition toward a regenerative economy of life, sacredness, and caring rooted in communitarian values and deep respect for our mother Earth.

SAL practices and promotes food sovereignty and agroecology in alignment with over 200 million smallholder food producers articulated in the international peasant movement La Vía Campesina. Through community-based farming and movement-building, we sow seeds of resistance against agribusiness and cultivate our rights as peasants and workers. We feed our peoples and strengthen local-to-global solidarity in order to change the world!

Each growing season, SAL mobilizes to plant, weed, and harvest our heirloom corn and beans, as well as a variety of squash, all grown in the same field. We often plant red corn seeds on one side of the plot and white seeds on the other.

We previously knew these two varieties as Bloody Butcher and Hickory King, but cross-pollination has naturally produced R3R, which in its totality expresses a wide variety of kernel shapes and patterns, a range of cob sizes, and joyful array of colors. Wonderful surprises happen with intentional and grateful opening of each ear.

SAL works in community. We eat together too, though the pandemic has greatly limited our ability to celebrate through community events for relationship-building, popular education, and recruitment.

Coronavirus-related emergency orders issued in Puerto Rico during March 2020 compelled me to leave the archipelago, where I had been working informally as a farm apprentice for several weeks. I returned home to Kentucky, soon finding employment at a diversified two-family farm. I was allotted a small plot of land for subsistence production, in addition to my wage for full-time work between April and December.

Once my employer prepared the plot days before the summer solstice, my sowing of corn and beans began. My planting technique combined skills acquired through years of involvement in SAL with lessons learned through personal gardening efforts and, more importantly, by working with peasants in Latin America and the Caribbean. My experience of the peasant-to-peasant methodology for scaling agroecology has thus entailed the spontaneous sharing of knowledge and more structured learning.

I planted R3R in the first half of the plot and two Central American varieties of corn in the back. My natural farming experimentation involved planting only blue R3R seeds in front section and a unique red seed towards the middle. With pole beans intercropped among three rows of corn and bush beans densely planted at the edge of the field, I succeeded with developing a small agroecological paradise, enjoyed by myself, both families on the farm, and visitors.

The first weeding loosened the soil following days of heavy rain. The second weeding a week later involved light mounding and hilling with a hoe to provide support to the plants. Less than a month after planting, squash entered my plot from the side, compelling me to reposition the vines in order to prevent them from dominating the space.

Two fascinating phenomena occurred on several corn stalks at multiple times during August and September. Nitrogen-fixing aerial root mucilage formed after heavy rain. Huitlacoche grew abundantly as well.

Historical memory and collective action are truly necessary to achieve a Just Transition toward a regenerative economy of life, sacredness, and caring rooted in communitarian values and deep respect for our mother Earth.

—TYLER SHORT

Tassels grew about two months after planting. Harvest commenced with chilote, or baby corn. In late September, the dry bean harvest began. I waited for the corn to mature, but around the equinox, I had little patience.

By late October, all of the R3R was dry enough for harvest and processing, which occurred in stages. My brother assisted me with removing corn ear worms from the tip of each of the cobs.

The corn stored from my personal production will likely sustain me for an entire year. I also have plenty of seed for planting and sharing to advance the Adopt a Seed action as part of La Via Campesina's campaign Seed Heritage of the People for the Good of Humanity.

Tyler Short (he/him)

Tyler is a young peasant and worker organized in the Youth Articulation of La Via Campesina North America.

43

Jardines de Pandemia

Palabras por Delia Pinto-Santini; Artes por Sam Shafer

Comparto aquí la historia de un jardín que nació del caos. Un cambio inesperado, una sacudida en nuestras rutinas, le recordó a mi familia cuán vulnerable es nuestro acceso a los alimentos. Nos recordó que, en nuestras actuales condiciones de vida, solo tenemos la posibilidad de adquirir alimentos cuando recibimos un sueldo producto de nuestro trabajo. Si por alguna razón no hay trabajo remunerado entonces no hay un sistema que nos permita el acceso a la comida o si lo hay, no sería de la mejor calidad. Uno a menudo no tiene el espacio mental de ponerse a pensar siquiera qué tipo de alimentos estamos sujetos a adquirir en los mercados, que tan frescos están cuando los adquirimos, de donde vienen o por qué comemos unos alimentos sobre otros. La situación de vernos inmovilizados en casa nos permitió mirar desde el caos una realidad subyacente que a menudo podemos suprimir. ¿Qué pasaría si no pudiésemos comprar alimentos? ¿Qué pasaría si hubiese escasez de estos en las tiendas? Nos dimos cuenta de nuestra vulnerabilidad en el actual modelo socioeconómico en el cual la alimentación, una buena alimentación, no está disponible equilibradamente para todos.

¿Qué hacer? Como por arte de magia, el universo inició su trabajo. Viviendo en un apartamento rentado, en el medio de la ciudad y sin tener tierras disponibles alrededor, decidimos "adueñarnos" de las jardineras del edificio, las cuales tenían algunas plantas ornamentales y unos buenos espacios vacíos entre ellas. Había también una jardinera exterior por la ventana de nuestra sala, a la cual no le habíamos prestado atención. En los pocos años que llevábamos en este edificio, algunas veces durante el verano, la gerencia sembraba allí algunas flores. Esta jardinera había estado vacía por un tiempo, con tan solo una planta de menta que una vecina había sembrado en uno de los extremos, y como buena menta, crecía y se esparcía ávidamente. Le contamos de nuestro plan a unos pocos vecinos, quienes respondieron: "¿Cómo? ¡La gerencia del edificio les va a decir que no, que estos no son espacios para sembrar comida! Les van a quitar las plantas." Hicimos caso omiso, decidimos asumir la filosofía de pedir perdón antes que pedir permiso! ¡E hicimos bien!

En un paseo con mi hijo, pasamos por el frente de una casa donde habían dejado plantitas de flores Zinnia para llevar GRATIS. Nos llevamos tres plantitas cuyas raíces encontrarían hogar en la jardinera de la ventana. Nos fuimos a la tienda de jardines y nos encontramos con una variedad de tomates: cherry, 'Cherokee red' y 'yellow pear'. Y finalmente conseguimos sobrecitos de semillas de arúgula, perejil, cilantro y albahaca. Para ayudar con el suelo, adquirimos unos pequeños sacos de tierra y abono. Que emoción fue enriquecer el suelo, proveer el espacio para que las semillas expresaran su potencial. Para los tomates construimos soportes con palos de bambú que nos regalaron unos amigos. Empezó entonces el nexo de amor con las semillas y lo que serían, con las plantulitas y su crecimiento; un compromiso se había creado con el cuidado del jardín. ¡Ahora hay algo que hacer en las mañanas y las tardes! Proveer agua para que las plantas sigan creciendo y las semillas germinen. ¡¡Cuando empiezan a salir las plantulitas, que alegría!! Cada tipo de semilla germinando a su ritmo, unas primeras y otras después. Las arúgulas más rápidamente y la albahaca un poco retrasada. El aprendizaje no se hace esperar: creemos que el suelo donde estaban las albahacas estuvo muy rocoso. ¡Quizás el próximo año podríamos empezar la albahaca en semilleros y luego pasarlas

a la jardinera! Las exclamaciones de los vecinos no se hicieron esperar: "¿Cómo van los tomates? ¡Ahí van las plantitas! ¡Qué bella flor!" Cuando floreció la primera flor de Zinnia, una niña del edificio quería arrancarla y llevarla a su casa. ¡Le dijimos que era bonito dejar las flores en la planta, porque así todos las podríamos disfrutar y durarán también mucho más! Estábamos creando un mayor sentido de comunidad. Estamos generando conversaciones y conexiones entre los vecinos. ¡Y todo con un pequeño jardín!

La vida del jardín trajo más vida: empiezas a ver el suelo vivo con muchos insectos. Cuando llegaron las flores, llegaron mariposas. ¡¡Un día llegaron unos gusanitos verdes que se comieron la mayoría de las arúgulas ya casi a punto de cosechar!! Estas 'plaguitas' también tienen espacio en la rueda de la vida; esto nos reconectó con la idea de pensar en cómo controlarlas y darles su espacio sin químicos que las maten, y que a la vez matan el suelo. Quizás debemos cosechar la arúgula más pronto antes de que atraigan a los gusanitos o cosechar tan pronto aparezcan los gusanitos y dejarles algunas como regalo. ¡En las plantas de tomate empezamos a ver telas de araña! ¡Y un día vimos un pequeño 'slug' y un ciempiés encima de un tomate! Me remonté a la infancia donde todo esto me maravillaba, asombraba y me hacía sentir feliz. El cuidado del jardín, dió espacio para la meditación, mientras regaba las plantas o veía las nuevas hojas crecer, los frutos aparecer, las flores florecer, reconecté con mi madre y su jardín, recordé los olores de la infancia, las cestitas de tomate cherry que nos sentábamos a comer mi hermana y yo, las tardes estudiando en un pupitre debajo del árbol de mango, las subidas para recoger los mangos más altos, el árbol de onoto, la iguana en el árbol de semeruco que orinó a mi papá mientras leía el periódico, los nidos de pajaritos escondidos en el árbol de Ficus y en las palmas de coco enano. Este pequeño jardín de la pandemia traía a la vida mis recuerdos, y se convertía en otra memoria que ahora mi hijo podía vivir y recordar.

Después de todo, !si podemos producir comida! El jardín nos trajo hermosos recuerdos de lo que fuimos, somos y seremos. Nada se pierde y el conocimiento que llevamos en nuestras psiquis y nuestros cuerpos puede siempre ser llamado y accionado.

Así pasó el verano y ya se sentía la llegada del otoño, cuando supe entonces a través de la pérdida, lo mucho que este pequeño jardín me traía de regalo, el nexo tan grande que había creado con este espacio de vida. Mi hijo me despertó esa mañana diciendo: ¡¡Mamá hay alguien limpiando la jardinera, han sacado todas las plantas!! No lo podía creer, fue como si un ciclón hubiese pasado, el sentimiento de pérdida era grande. La persona me dijo que había sido enviado a limpiar todas las 'malezas' de la jardinera... Oh no!! ¿Cómo podían decir que eran malezas? ¡¡Eran flores y hierbas!! Entendí que después de todo ya era tiempo de dejar ir el jardín, lista o no, se cerraba un ciclo.

No importa que lo que hagamos pueda ser considerado 'maleza' por algunos. Aunque nuestros jardines parezcan difíciles de crear o mantener, aunque en un principio no sepamos qué hacer, aunque muchos los destruyan, accidentalmente o intencionalmente, siempre habrá valido la pena sembrar una semilla. Es con este espíritu que me alisto para las dificultades y alegrías por venir, para la posibilidad de mantener vivos jardines metafóricos y tangibles con la guía de los que vinieron antes, para que siga habiendo suelo fértil para los que vendrán después. *Happy growing!!*

Delia Pinto-Santini (she/her)

Delia has lived for the last 20 years in the Pacific Northwest. She grew up in Venezuela. She is a mom, partner, friend, daughter, sister, biomedical worker. Most of the time she is an optimistic, long-time learner. She loves walks, hikes and camping with son and friends. She likes dancing and laughing. She has loved learning from and with CAGJ friends this last year.

Sam Shafer (she/her)

Sam is a white, Jewish, early childhood educator and inconsistent creative living on occupied Duwamish land. You can usually find Sam admiring lichen and mud puddles, riding her bike, or cooking delightfully weird meals.

Borikén:
I Can Hear Her Breathing

By Maria Elena Rodriguez

A Puerto Rican who has always lived in the diaspora, I made my way to the island permanently in 2017, determined to make good on my years-long desire of farming in Borikén—the indigenous name for Puerto Rico. While 2020 brought unimaginable struggles into communities around the world, it also saw the sprouting, the growth of my long-held dream.

My partner and I recently purchased a farm here in Rio Grande, Puerto Rico—an 8-acre parcel of steep, rocky land that slopes and undulates down to the river that serves as a boundary line. The farm sits at the edge of the El Yunque rainforest with its nearly daily torrential downpours, its slick, clay soils, and an ever-present cacophony of tropical nature sounds playing like a soundtrack in the background.

As I dream of the possibilities of this land, envisioning my new path forward, I am reminded of how we got here—of all that has happened.

This island has experienced so much. It has experienced *too* much.

> 400 years of Spanish colonial rule followed by another 100 of the U.S. variety.

> A brutal political campaign that squashed a movement for Independence in the 1950's, making it illegal for a time to fly the Puerto Rican flag or speak Spanish.

> An economy plunged into bankruptcy by crushing, un-payable debt, and the 2016 PROMESA Act that imposed austerity measures and gutted the island's healthcare, public services, infrastructure, and education systems.

> Hurricane Maria's landfall on September 20th, 2017 that destroyed infrastructure, the entire electrical and communications grid, and an estimated 80% of local food production and claimed the lives of more than 4,600 people.

> A 6.4 magnitude earthquake on January 7th, 2020, and subsequent aftershocks that lasted months, displacing over 8,000 people from their homes.

And now…. the COVID-19 pandemic that is raging across the densely-populated island, adding pressure to an already-fragile healthcare system that is buckling under these new demands, this "new normal."

This past year has me thinking about the power of seeds. I remember overhearing a local farm leader recount how an elder had told them that the best way to store seeds—these time cap-sules of flavor, of nourishment, of culture—is *in fact* the soil. To cultivate the land, sow those cherished seeds, harvest and savor the fruit, save *their* seeds, and start the cycle all over again—that is our best hope for food sovereignty. It is our best hope for local control and self-determination of our food heritage, now and in the future. I am reminded of my seed storage box in the bottom of my

fridge—complete with a few straggling seed packs leftover from donation efforts in the aftermath of Hurricane Maria. I make a mental note to plant more seeds, to sow as much as I can. Even if the farm beds are not yet completed, the soil is forgiving and appreciative.

When I leave the island for "the States," I inevitably end up answering prodding questions about our experience surviving Hurricane Maria or the recent earthquakes. I hear that tired refrain repeated over and over: "Puerto Ricans have dealt with so much. They are so resilient."

I'm tired of being resilient. We are tired of *having* to be resilient.

My barrio—the entire island, really—is littered with casualties of these disasters, sometimes natural but *always* man-made. It is strewn with houses that used to be homes but are now barren, empty, crumbling. Tattered blue FEMA tarps dot the landscape and sway like flags flapping in the wind. Tangled green vines and grasses climb over fences, up walls, and over roofs, choking out the dazzling sunlight and building new microclimates, creating new realms. The natural world marches on, chugs forward with its unrelenting hum, enveloping our puny, human-sized structures, our best attempts at forever... swallowing them whole.

Back on our farm I clear a small patch of land of its vines and grasses. I prepare the soil and tuck the seeds into the welcoming ground. I don't bother to water the seeds because I know the timely rainforest downpour is on its way. As I look out over the land I am now entrusted to steward—with its sweltering breezes and raucous birdsong that I cannot yet identify—the words of Indian author and political activist Arundhati Roy ring in my ears:

> *"Another world is not only possible, she is on her way.*
> *On a quiet day, I can hear her breathing."*

Maria Elena Rodriguez (she/her)

Maria Elena is a former Co-Coordinator of the CAGJ Food Justice Project. She is a Food Systems Specialist with DAISA Enterprises where she conducts research, provides strategic assistance to foundations and nonprofits, and supports emerging food leaders. She is also the Founder of Cosecha Caribe, an agroecological farm and food business. She is committed to creating a food system that honors ancestral knowledge, uplifts BIPOC communities, nourishes the environment, and deepens Queer community.

A Recipe for A Resilient Global Economy

By Hillary Haden

February 1, 2019

Tonight, while munching on sourdough crackers flavored with rosemary, I sat through a graduate school class called Disaster Relief and Development. My professor stands in the front of a bland white room in front of a white board, his powerpoint slides projected up in front of us with the word RESILIENCE written across the title slide's mid-section. For academics in the field of Community Development, resilience means thinking ahead of time about what shocks might hit a system and planning ahead for those shocks rather than cleaning up afterwards. Academics like to apply it to housing in places where there are tsunamis or hurricanes and to thinking about public health infrastructure in the case of a pandemic which we haven't even had in a century now. But today, when I told my professor I thought the whole global economy would benefit from thinking more about resilience in supply chains or resilience in terms of economic means for citizens who might undergo crises, he gave me a weird look and said "well, that's one idea" and continued on with the lecture. To me, having a diverse set of sources of things we know we all need instead of hollowing out the supply chain so it runs through one country makes a lot of sense. So does the idea of making sure families have extra money to put away to handle a crisis like losing a job or someone in the family getting sick.

June 20, 2019

I run a nonprofit that works on trade policy. This week for work I've been doing research into our supply chains for chemicals we use to make pharmaceuticals because we learned that China controls roughly 80% of the supply chain. So much of the rhetoric around China right now is really difficult to take in because it's so nationalist. It's almost like "China" has become a buzzword for political leaders in the US—like China has become a boogeyman for US problems. There's plenty to criticize about the workers' rights track record in China, but I wish sometimes that people could articulate their issues without staking "them" and "us" value statements. In reality, I don't care that China has the medical supply chain, except that it's a recipe for disaster that we might someday need several sources of those goods. In the US, we've just started hearing about the Uighurs in detail, and we're trying to find out if any of the supply chain runs through places where they're using forced labor. It's been really hard to get members of Congress to listen to us as we've been trying to do educational work around the issue. As an organizer, the cynical part of my mind wonders what kind of shock it will take to get people in power to care.

November 30, 2019

20 years ago today 80,000 people gathered in the streets of Seattle to stop the World Trade Organization from reaching its ugly tentacles further into our everyday lives. The WTO wanted to control decisions about the food we eat, the medicines we take, and the environmental regulations we're allowed to pass. The most impressive part about this organizing is that it continues to this day, and it has largely stopped the WTO from being able to grow even though we still feel its power when we try to do things like fight climate change or make new public health regulations. In those moments, the WTO shows up and lets us know we're not following the golden rules of its global economy. It's been really interesting to reflect on the ways the rhetoric has changed. My generation wants to engage with other countries, but we want to do it in a way that protects our workers, environment and food systems instead of giving that power away to greedy, unaccountable trans-national corporations. Millennials generally have a paradigm that puts people against corporations rather than the US against China or Mexico. Even though the WTO hasn't moved forward, thousands of trade agreements have, and we're seeing the impacts and destabilization from it as people like Jair Bolsonaro, Donald Trump, Boris Johnson, and others win elections.

March 1, 2020

Things are really uncertain just now. Two days ago, the first person in the US died of coronavirus—a new virus that began in China in December—here in Seattle. People are panicking and buying all the hand sanitizer and food that they can from the store. When we went, it was all gone, and my parents decided to send me some from Iowa. All my meetings for this week have been cancelled or moved online. As I work, I'm baking oregano-flavored sourdough crackers with flour we found on a shelf in the garage after we looked at 3 different grocery stores. Cooking is a recipe for success when I need to take my mind off something. Our unreliable narrator of a President says we'll be down to zero cases soon.

June 8, 2020

Today, after nearly 3 months trapped at home, we learned that we'll be slowly allowed to re-open parts of the economy. I can't stop thinking about a conversation I had with a professor in graduate school about how if a big disaster came, families wouldn't be prepared with rent money or healthcare. This pandemic is the perfect storm for a country that demands we continue tying healthcare to employment. People are losing their jobs and then their healthcare in a moment when having healthcare could very easily mean life or death. We've got an eviction moratorium because so many folks can't pay rent. We've hollowed out our medical supply chains to the point that we have no personal protective equipment for nurses, let alone people outside the healthcare system. About a week ago, someone from the Trump administration put forward a plan to bring some of our medical supply and device manufacturing back to the US. It's a far cry from a worker-centered proposal that I'd advocate for, but I think people are waking up to the economic mess we've created for ourselves. I guess the question remains, will they fix it? Post-coronavirus, will they create a system that situates people to be economically stable? Or, will we return to the business as usual, volatile economy of the past that puts corporations first and people and the planet last?

It was an incredibly difficult decision, but this is the first year I haven't spent Christmas at home with my family baking cookies and playing music and staying up late. I'm thankful to have a partner whose family lives close. We spent our Christmas eating empanadas, reading books, and going for walks—which I suppose is a very good second best to Christmas in Iowa with my family. Some days it's hard to feel hopeful that we'll come out of corona-virus better than we started, but other days, the sun peeks its way out through the clouds. 2020 politicized so many people. There are people working to significantly expand the social safety net, working to rebuild the domestic economy in ways that are more forward-looking, and people who are really looking out for each other in this space. All of those things give me a hope that we may be headed for some kind of new normal where our policies, values, and lives align more clearly.

Check out Hillary's recipe for Sourdough Crackers on page 124!

Recipe for a Disastrous Global Economy

2 cups corporate control

1 cup unsustainable resource usage

2 TBSP worker exploitation

Mix thoroughly. Batter might separate, but keep mixing. Even when it continues to not mix well, just keep stirring and hoping it turns out okay. If your guests don't like it, tell them they don't have taste and that they should buck up and swallow it.

Recipe for a Stable Global Economy

1 cup good jobs

2 cups climate support

As much democratic control over food and health systems as you can fold into the mix

2 TBSP cooperation

1 TBSP hope

Mix jobs, climate support, and democratic control. Add regulation as necessary. Fold hope and cooperation all the way through the batter. Remove exploitation every time it bubbles to the top of the dough. Cook thoroughly and serve among friends.

Hillary Haden (she/her)

Hillary is the Director at the Washington Fair Trade Coalition. Her love for people-centered economic development led her to Havana, Cuba for her Masters' Degree research in Community Development. She lives in Redmond, WA, with her dog Scout, and is a hiker, a reader, and a home-made bread maker.

Cornhusk dolls lay on grass

By Maegan McCoy

Check out Maegan's recipe for Pickled Onions and read her bio on page 119!

Strong Roots

Simone Adler (they/them)

Simone organizes in the food sovereignty movement (previously CAGJ's organizing director 2016-20; currently organizing co-director at Pesticide Action Network). Outside of campaigns to transform the food system, Simone brings their white, queer & Jewish identities to political education & solidarity organizing for Palestinian self-determination and to end white supremacy. They play klezmer clarinet in Shpilkis (shpilkisseattle.com), make art on revolution & spirituality, and live on Duwamish land.

STRONG COMMUNITIES are the ROOTS OF RESILIENCE.

Recipe for White Vegan(ism) & Self-Portrait of a White Vegan

By Ayana Naomi

There are many shades to veganism, with White veganism being a watered-down, neoliberal shade. There are also many reasons to compel others toward veganism: lessen your contribution to climate change, improve your own health, or save animals. However, I believe these rationales to be distracting and White veganism to be an adulteration of the true essence of veganism: abolition. White veganism upholds the patriarchy and racism that keeps animals and humans oppressed. I want no part of this veganism.

This recipe is a satire highlighting the counterintuitive and extremely harmful narratives White veganism espouses. The second image is a reflection of the personal work to pursue the liberation of all beings. As a White vegan of 10 years, I am compelled to veganism as a protest to capitalist, industrialized agriculture and have the privilege to access the resources to manifest this protest in my diet everyday. Dietary changes are a minuscule part of the overhaul abolitionist veganism requires of the entire food system though. What I am cultivating in my own home, building up slowly and full of nutrients, like soil, is a humble understanding that we are all interconnected, that revolution is evolution, and abolitionist veganism is one part of the food sovereign future I envision.

Recipe for White Veganism

PREP TIME: length of one PETA video

The most easily digestible form of
veganism you can whip up with
these six easy tropes to fall into.
Can be easily doubled for twice
the white supremacy)!

Ingredients

1 C dogmatic belief humans
are the worst (source
ingredients from Half Earth)

2 C Igore connected
oppressions rooted in
racial capitalism

2 Tbsp offensive comparisons
to slavery, rape, & the
Holocaust

1 Tbsp still participating
in industrial food system

1 tsp driving past poor
Black, Indigenous, Latino/a
communities where CAFOs are
concentrated to film
atrocious animal suffering

Dash white savior complex
(optional)

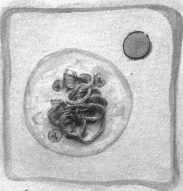

Instructions

1. Combine active
opposition to Indigenous
sovereignty & green
capitalism into one
bowl

2. Bake in silence
around farmworker
rights

3. Enjoy feeling that
veganism is THE
solution!

ana Naomi 2021

mutual aid

libnation of all beings

prioritize joy

local whole FOODS

solitude

Black, Latino/a & Indigenous Food Sovereignty

LandBack & land stewards not owners

SLOWing down

self medicating and selfcare?

Ayana Naomi ©

64

Ayana Naomi (she/her)

I am a Master's student studying agroecology and food systems policy as well as a Museum Studies Fellow on the land of the Anishinaabek where the University of Michigan resides. I hope to collaboratively create aspirational, maginative spaces of activism and food sovereignty education outdoors. As a settler and vegan (going on 10 years now) I strive for continual self-relfexivity and liberation for all beings from capitalism and colonial structures.

Being in Movement Spaces Together: Thoughts, Feelings and Desires from a Local Abolitionist

By Avery Temple

SIBLINGS IN ARMS, WHY ARE WE FIGHTING AGAIN?

quit aiming your gun at me.

can't you see that we are the dogs, pitted
against one another? we ought to be
biting the owner, not each other.

i want to be dancing in the streets with you.
busting open cop car windows with you.
making soup for you. breathing life into what
it means to live within poetry with you.

it is scary, i know. it's one punch after the
other. it is too much time spent in pain.
it is layers of brick on our chest, it is the scent
of heavy death following us in our sleep.

THAT YOU
DON'T HAVE TO
FEEL ALL
ALONE.

we are mourning the futures we will never
have, the children we refuse to bear. we are
righteous anger shielding deep blue grief.

we are turning on each other out of fear.

TRUST IN US AND CREATE A HOME.

it will not be perfect.

not the first time or the first thousand times. we
will have to talk, learn how to give and receive
feedback, soothe and soften, reassess. we will
have to be willing to grow beyond our ego..

but we cannot break through to the next
world with only one set of hands.

AND WE MUST LEARN HOW TO BELONG TO EACH OTHER AGAIN.

so be brave and let us try.

Avery Temple (they/she)

Avery Temple (they/she) is a queer, multi-racial Latinx and community
organizer. She feels most at home within movements that center
climate, racial, economic, and transformative justice but is passionate
about all people-powered spaces that center life. She is a facilitator,
abolitionist, writer, lover of the arts, and eager student of all teachers
who are practicing joyful militancy.

Community Fridges on Every Corner

I've heard there is a fear

of taco trucks on every corner.

Yet another tired call for tighter borders.

How is it that

their hearts

have yet to get

any **WARMER?**

Do they *NOT SEE* the way public manifestations of love

have only made us stronger?

Community fridges on every corner
Inspired by the philosophies and free meals of
yonder year's Black Panthers
Ensuring radical love and care is forevermore
When it comes to love, we recognize no
ceilings, only the floor

There is always more
To give and to do
To imagine and to see through
Collective protection and nourishment
our krazy glue

In a way, this pandemic has given power back to the people. The facade of a government 'for the people,' has finally come down in the eyes of our communities, which have unfortunately bore the brunt of negligence and inadequate support from the State. And so, we have taken care into our own hands. To a certain extent, we always have. But, this pandemic has really heightened the need for community care, for protecting and nourishing our own, because we have very blatantly been shown that the State will not. With a greater need, we stepped up. We took the premise of "we protect us," to food insecurity, and we relied on local businesses to let us plug in (quite literally), to help the fridges stay running; we turned to those with more, with any level of abundance, and asked for donations in either food, money, or time, and we showed up for each other.

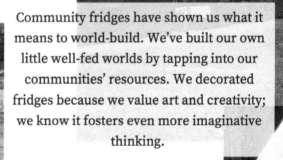

Take what you need, leave what you don't. We have enough. This planet has enough for all of us. The State is that entity which has imposed this notion of scarcity, partly because they profit off of it if they hoard goods and sell it back to us, and partly because they are actually using up resources inappropriately and lacking a future-oriented mindset.

Community fridges have shown us what it means to world-build. We've built our own little well-fed worlds by tapping into our communities' resources. We decorated fridges because we value art and creativity; we know it fosters even more imaginative thinking.

Skeptics wondered how long these community fridges would last. "How long will they continue to care for each other like this???" they mused from their penthouse apartments. We sure showed them. We will continue to show them. In tapping into community and building up and nourishing each other in this way, through this manifestation of public love and care, we have stepped into the portal.

See Ayling's recipe for
Memelas on page 96!

Ayling Zulema Dominguez (she/they)

Ayling is a first-generation Chicana-Dominicana with roots in many places. As a poet, creative, and youth arts educator in an abolitionist mindset, her work is the stuff of forging community; of affirming belonging as the first step toward liberation; of imagining new, better and more radically loving worlds. Her writing and creative work do not only celebrate joyful resistance, but also push her readers to actively oppose systems of oppression. Instagram: @rhymeswithmean

If the trees on my farmland could speak

By Amanpreet Sidhu

ਜੇ ਮੇਰੇ ਖੇਤਾਂ ਦੇ ਦਰਖਤ ਗੱਲ ਕਰ ਸਕਦੇ,
ਤਾਂ ਪੁੱਛਦੇ।

ਪੋਹ ਦੀਆਂ ਠੰਢੀਆਂ ਰਾਤਾਂ ਵੱਿਚ
ਕਸਿਾਨ ਕਿਉ ਉੱਤਰ ਆਏ ਸੜਕਾਂ ਤੇ
ਆਮ ਕਰਕੇ ਤਾਂ ਇਹ ਐਨੀ ਦਨਿੀ
ਦੇਸ਼ ਦੀ ਭੁੱਖ ਮਟਾਉਣ ਲਈ ਕਣਕਾਂ ਨੂੰ ਪਹਲਿਾ
ਪਾਣੀ ਲਾਉਣ ਲਈ ਨਕਿਲ ਦਾ ਆ।

ਪਰ ਇਹ ਤਾਂ ਇੰਝ ਲੱਗਦੇ ਕਿ ਕਸਿੇ ਮਹਾਨ
ਯਾਤਰਾ ਤੇ ਚੱਲੇ ਹੋਣ।

ਉਸ ਯਾਤਰਾ ਤੇ ਜੁੱਥੇ ਘਰ ਬੈਠਣਾ ਪਾਪ ਹੋਵੇ।
ਉਸ ਯਾਤਰਾ ਤੇ ਜੋ ਹਰ ਵਰਗ ਦੀ ਸਾਂਝੀ ਹੋਵੇ।
ਉਸ ਯਾਤਰਾ ਤੇ ਜੋ ਸਭ ਧਰਮਾਂ ਦੀ ਸਾਂਝੀ ਹੋਵੇ।
ਉਸ ਯਾਤਰਾ ਤੇ ਜੱਥੇ ਕਰਿਤ ਕਸਿਾਨੀ ਹੀ ਧਰਮ
ਹੋਵੇ।

ਜੇ ਮੇਰੇ ਖੇਤਾਂ ਦੇ ਦਰੱਖਤ ਗੱਲ ਕਰ ਸਕਦੇ,
ਤਾਂ ਦੱਸਦੇ।

ਕੇ ਸਨਿਮਾ ਸਕੋਪ ਦੇ ਹਰੇ ਭਰੇ ਖੇਤਾਂ ਵੱਿਚ
ਪਤਾ ਨੀ, ਕਨਿੇ ਕਸਿਾਨਾਂ ਨੂੰ ਕਨਿੇ ਦਹਾਕੇ ਲੱਗ
ਗਏ ਰੰਗ ਭਰ ਦਆਿਂ।

ਪਤਾ ਨੀ, ਕਨਿੇ ਪਾਟੇ ਹੱਥਾਂ ਦੀਆ ਵਆਿਈਆਂ
ਬਣ ਗਈਆਂ ਖੇਤਾਂ ਦੇ ਰਾਜੇ ਦੀ ਪਾਟੀ ਕਸਿਮਤ।

ਪਤਾ ਨੀ, ਕਨਿੇ ਪੈਰਾਂ ਨੇ ਮਦੀਆਂ
ਸੱਪਾਂ ਦੀਆਂ ਸਰਿੀਆਂ,
ਦੇਸ਼ ਦੀ ਭੁੱਖ ਮਟਾਉਣ ਲਈ।

ਪਤਾ ਨੀ, ਇੰਨਾ ਕਨਿੀਆਂ ਕਾਲੀਆਂ ਸਰਦ ਰਾਤਾਂ
ਹੰਢਾਇਆ,
ਦੇਸ਼ ਦੇ ਉੱਜਵਲ ਭਵਖਿ ਲਈ।

ਜੇ ਮੇਰੇ ਖੇਤਾਂ ਦੇ ਦਰੱਖਤ ਗੱਲ ਕਰ ਸਕਦੇ,
ਤਾਂ ਦੱਸਦੇ ਕਸਿਾਨ ਦਾ ਹਾਲ।

ਕਿ ਇਸ ਭੋਲੇ ਨੂੰ ਸਮਝ ਨੀ ਸੀ ਆਉਂਦੀ,
ਖੂਨ ਨੂੰ ਪਸੀਨਾਂ ਕਰਨ ਤੇ ਵੀ,
ਖੈਤ ਜ਼ੰਹਰਿ ਕਿਉ ਉਗਲਣ ਲੱਗ ਪਏ।

ਕਿ ਇਸ ਭੋਲੇ ਨੂੰ ਸਮਝ ਨੀ ਸੀ ਆਉਂਦੀ,
ਕਿ ਮੇਰੇ ਪੁੱਤਾਂ ਹੁੱਸਿ ਹੀ ਕਿਉ ਆਈ,
ਖੇਤ ਤੇ ਸਰੱਹਦ ਦੀ ਰਾਖੀ।

ਕਿ ਇਸ ਭੋਲੇ ਨੂੰ ਸਮਝ ਨੂੰ ਸੀ ਆਉਂਦੀ,
ਕਿ ਨਵੇਂ ਵਪਾਰੀੀ ਕੱਫਣਾਂ ਚੋਂ ਵੀ
ਕਵਿੇਂ ਮੁਨਾਫਾ ਖੱਟ ਜਾਂਦੇ ਆ।

ਕਿ ਇਸ ਭੋਲੇ ਨੂੰ ਸਮਝ ਨੀ ਸੀ ਆਉਂਦੀ,
ਕਿ ਧੀ ਦੇ ਵਆਿਹ ਦਾ ਫਕਿਰ ਮੱਥੇ ਦੀਆਂ
ਝੁਰੜੀਆਂ ਕਿਉ ਡੂੰਘੀਆਂ ਕਰੀ ਜਾਂਦਾ।

ਕਿ ਇਸ ਭੋਲੇ ਨੂੰ ਸਮਝ ਨੀ ਸੀ ਆਉਂਦੀ,
ਕਿ ਕਰਜੇ ਵਾਲੂੰ ਫੰਨੀਅਰ,
ਉਸ ਨੂੰ ਹੀ ਕਿਉ ਬਾਰ ਬਾਰ ਡੰਗੀ ਜਾਂਦਾ।

ਜੇ ਮੇਰੇ ਖੇਤਾਂ ਦੇ ਦਰੱਖਤ ਗੱਲ ਕਰ ਸਕਦੇ,
ਤਾਂ ਦੱਸਦੇ।

ਇਸ ਬਾਰ ਇਸ ਨੂੰ ਨਵੀਆਂ ਪੁਰਾਣੀਆਂ ਚਾਲਾਂ
ਦੀ ਸਮਝ ਲੱਗਦੀੀ ਆ,
ਇਸ ਬਾਰ ਆਪਣੀ ਧਰਤ ਮਾਂ ਨੂੰ ਨੀ ਵਕਿਣ
ਦਦਿਾ ਨਵੇਂ ਵਪਾਰੀਆਂ ਦੇ ਹੱਥ।

....ਤਾਂ ਦੱਸਦੇ
ਇਸ ਯਾਤਰਾ ਚੋਂ ਹੀ ਜਿਉਂਦੇ ਰਹਿ ਦੀ ਉਮੀਦ
ਦਸਿਦੀ ਆ।
ਇਸ ਕਾਫਲੇ ਚੋਂ ਹੀ ਦਖਿਦਾ ਆਪਣੇ ਬੱਚਿਆਂ
ਦਾ ਬੇਹਤਰ ਭਵਖਿ।

ਜੇ ਮੇਰੇ ਖੇਤਾਂ ਦੇ ਦਰੱਖਤ ਗੱਲ ਕਰ ਸਕਦੇ,
ਤਾਂ ਦੱਸਦੇ।

ਇਨਾਂ ਤਾਂ ਕਰ ਲਆਿ ਫੈਸਲਾ
ਠੰਢੀਆਂ ਰਾਤਾਂ ਕੱਟਣ ਦਾ ਤਾਨਾਸ਼ਾਹ ਦੇ ਦਰ ਤੇ
ਇਨਾਂ ਤਾਂ ਕਰ ਲਆਿ ਫੈਸਲਾ
ਸਰਿਫ ਜਿੱਤ ਕੇ ਹੀ ਮੁੜਨ ਦਾ।

ਜੇ ਮੇਰੇ ਖੇਤਾਂ ਦੇ ਦਰੱਖਤ ਗੱਲ ਕਰ ਸਕਦੇ,
ਤਾਂ ਦੱਸਦੇ।
ਇਨਾਂ ਤਾਂ ਕਰ ਲਆਿ ਫੈਸਲਾ
ਸਰਿਫ ਜਿੱਤ ਕੇ ਹੀ ਮੁੜਨ ਦਾ।
ਸਰਿਫ ਤੇ ਸਰਿਫ ਜਿੱਤ ਕੇ ਹੀ ਮੁੜਨ ਦਾ।

75

Translation by Pukhraj Sidhu

If the trees on my farmland
could speak,
then they would ask
In the bitter cold nights of ਪੋਹ,
Why are these kisaan marching
down the roads
Instead of watering the
season's first crop
to provide for their fellow coun-
tryfolk?

Perhaps they are setting off on
a pilgrimage.
A pilgrimage in which staying
home is a sin,
a pilgrimage that belongs to
every religion,
To all of society.

If the trees on my farmland
could speak,
then they would tell you
about the generations of
farmers it took to
nourish today's lush green
Bollywood backdrops.
About all the hands that have
been calloused over,
the fate lines that have been
tampered with and torn,
to paint those picture-perfect
sceneries.

They would tell you about the
corporate world that disrupted
their rhyme of life.

Contaminated their land in the
name of a green revolution,
polluted their air in the name
of industrialization,
and posioned their waters in
the name of evolution.

If the trees on my farmlands
could speak,
Then they would tell you about
a farmer who has had enough.
About a kisaan who refuses to
let his motherland be bought
out and tampered with.

This pilgrimage has given him
hope,
shown him a better future for
his children,
a better future for his country.

If the trees on my farmland
could walk,
then they too would uproot
themselves
to protest at the doorstep of a
totalitarian government.

They too would refuse to
return home
without winning this fight.

Amanpreet Sidhu (he/him) and **Pukhraj Sidhu** (she/her)

Aman was raised on his family's farm in Punjab, India where he grew up immersed in kheti. 20 years ago, Aman became the first in his family to leave his ancestral land and immigrate to North America. He wrote this piece in response to the ongoing Indian Farmers' Protest.

Pukhraj is an ABCD (American-Born Confused Desi) who studies Human Centered Design & Engineering at the University of Washington. She penned the translation alongside her father and learned more about his youth in the process.

i'm left with barely any words to express

sitting abroad feeling helpless, added on to the stress

a wise woman once told me

'one prayer can change a feeling of impossible, wait and see'

i'm not really good with my words like my friends

i splash colours on a canvas till the paint ends

and till my mind feels cleansed

this painting is my way of expressing through many words

screaming, yelling, begging, pleading

praying and meditating

this is my way to address

with barely any words to be expressed.

—JASMINE KAUR BRAR

I Stand With Farmers

By Jasmine Kaur Brar

I stand with Farmers

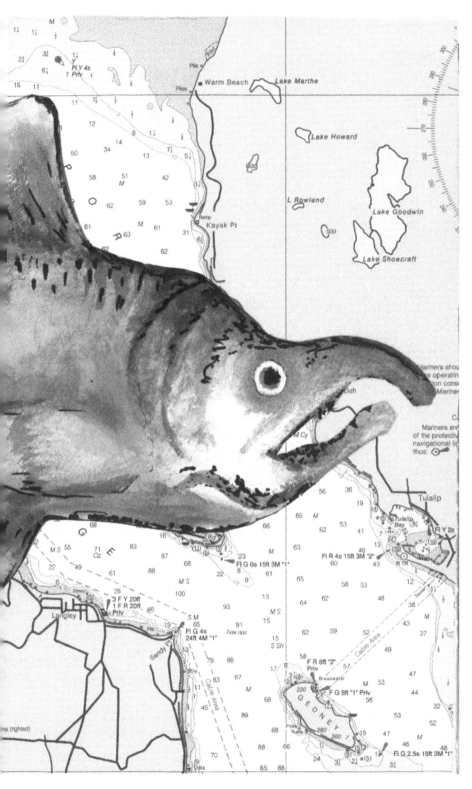

Chinook

By Kirsten Spooner

The image on the previous page portrays the intersection of indigenous food sovereignty and native habitat restoration. The original painting was made to be used as the flyer for an annual restoration party organized in collaboration with Duwamish Alive! at the Hamm Creek estuary along the Duwamish waterway. This area is vital in the reproductive cycle of salmon, making restoration extremely important. Every year salmon travel up river along the Duwamish to spawn in the protective estuaries. The Duwamish river is a working river, with various industries along its shore. In 2001 the EPA declared the lower Duwamish waterway a superfund site. Not only are salmon fighting against the pollutants caused by these industries, they are also affected by the destructive invasive species brought here by colonizers. For the purpose of restoring the estuary we clean up trash, remove invasive species, and plant native species. Unfortunately this year, due to Covid-19, we determined it would not be safe to organize the work party. In an effort to keep the spirit of the event alive, the original painting and prints were sold, with the entirety of the proceeds given to the Duwamish Longhouse.

Kirsten Spooner (she/her)

Occupied Duwamish Territory, anticapitalist abolitionist with a passion for printmaking. No gods, no masters, no borders. Currently involved in The Long Haul Mutual Aid Kitchen. Instagram: @Blackmountaindistro

Tasting the Stars

By Morgan Brown

Pray with your Salt
Poem for a Recipe:

She cooked with healing laughter tears and prayers
Songs and dances lived in her food
She kept a bent wood box in her heart
filled with spices that never ran out

My Grandmother still finds joy in feeding the world
through my hands her Love
whispering secrets to me through the bubbling soup
kissing my forehead with that steam
when I lean in to smell

xs'waanx, bilhaa, samii wun, smk'awtsi,
herring eggs, abalone, deer meat, oolichan grease
ada heelda maay
and so many berries
ada hoon, heelda hoon
and salmon, lots of salmon

The promises made
reverence even her cutting board knew
respecting the spirit of all who touched her blade

Abrupt
lost ones came searching
claiming to be the fathers of the found
banning our feasts
fearing the strength of Love
may turn to sand the dams in their hearts
dying salmon say it is true

84

Finding my way home
following her wooden spoon to the scent of cedar upriver
spawning salmon in the heart of my child

Way of life
binding us together
where the debt of gratitude is the gift of medicine

A pinch for your pocket
the spice she used most was timeless Love
inviting our tongues to reach all the way to the stars

Recipe in a Poem:

Pray with your salt
know the foods and medicines of your people
always thank them and care for them
let the different flavors of your tears
the rolling bubbles of your laughter
the healing medicine of your ancestors
be tasted by another

Morgan Brown (she/they)
I am a Queer Indigenous Tsimshian Ukrainian Mother. I work as the Protect Mother Earth Coordinator for the Swinomish Tribe. My inspiration and knowledge fall in the realms of Traditional Plant Medicine, First Foods, Indigenous Language Revitalization, Poetry, Healing Justice, Indigenous Childbirth Education, Motherhood, Healing Trauma through Indigenous Wisdom and partnering with Plants, Animals and Ancestors. I believe in Indigenous Women Leadership for the ReMatriation of Mother Earth.

Food Sovereignty, a Gift from Our Ancestors

By Demarus Tevuk

I was born in Nome, Alaska in a land free of fences. Without trees to block the view, the tundra, mountains, oceans, and rivers stretch out endlessly. It feels like all of my early childhood memories are of the country. Winters in the snow, ice fishing, sledding, playing in snow forts my dad made for us. Summers at fish camp, playing on the beach, gathering herbs under the bushes for my mom, picking blueberries and aqpik—in English they are known as cloudberries, plump orange clusters that glisten when ripe.

Looking back now, I took the freedom we had for granted. I returned home to Nome more frequently as a mother wishing to teach my children how to gather and how to love their ancestral homeland. We would explore abandoned houses and pick blueberries next to old Sourdough cabins. Gold prospectors and famous characters like Wyatt Earp come and go but our bonds to the tundra are eternal.

In our story of the creation of the drum, the last mother of the giant eagles mourns for the loss of her children. The Inupiat had no choice but to hunt the giant eagles to stop them from plucking whales out of the sea and only eating the tongues because this wasting of whales was starving the people. The giant eagle mother tells the hunter how to build the first drum and to play it as a reminder of her beating heart.

In my Indigenous worldview, time is cyclical and I see the pattern of heartache repeated in the European hunting of whales of the 1800's, driven to overharvest for commercial gain. Whales that fed us and shaped our culture of sharing nature's bounty were nearly exterminated. In Washington State, the Makah Tribe saw the whale population collapse and the tribe decided to suspend whaling until the whales were healthy again. For at least 70 years the Makah stopped their hunt, an entire lifetime of a generation lost as tools, songs, dances, and feasts sat silent.

On May 17, 1999 the Makah Tribe successfully landed a whale and the entire community celebrated as the gift of the whale was revitalized. The general public did not celebrate and more than 400 environmental and animal rights groups materialized to protest, led by people who were ignorant and fettered by their belief that the Save the Whales campaign of the 1970s should also apply to subsistence whale hunting.

I am eternally frustrated by the ignorance of these groups in their interpretation of what matters to Indigenous whaling cultures. During the subsistence whaling moratorium of 1977, a concerned group in California understood that the loss of hunting would be devastating to the northern Native Alaskan communities where western packaged foods are highly priced. The group thought that what the Inupiat communities were going to miss, that what was central to their culture, was the act of killing large animals. They proposed the shipment of live cattle that the Inupiat hunters could kill upon arrival.

For the general public to believe that Indigenous hunters enjoy killing animals is a gross and disgusting interpretation. I grew up with stories of the reverence we must show to the animals that feed us, that we must thank them and pray to them immediately, and that hunters are even taught to apologize the moment that they strike. The act of killing is done out of necessity, not out of what I can only guess these non-Indigenous groups think hunting means (something related to ego, perhaps; or connected to a sense of control of nature, which is also foreign to Indigenous cultures).

Ignorance and arrogance were repeated again in 1999 when Sea Shepherd created a racist campaign calling for violence against the Makah's reassertion of their treaty right to hunt grey whales. The pattern of the general public not understanding several key facts related to subsistence whaling is something that will be repeated until the public's attitude towards wanting to govern and assimilate Indigneous people disappears and the attitude of cultural superiority is replaced with empathy.

Food sovereignty is, sadly, something that we must define and protect because of the history of an oppressive culture forcibly removing the inherent rights of others to pray, grow, gather, hunt,

fish, feed, share, and care for themselves. For me, food sovereignty means cultural revitalization and continuing to support the treaty rights and other legal ways that our ancestors ensured our rights to care for ourselves.

As Native People, we have a duty to follow Natural Law above all else. I teach my children to feel thankfulness while gathering berries, to feel awe and wonder at the bounty that covers the hillsides and valleys, to respect the plants and animals, to take home only what we need for ourselves and for our gifts to share with friends and family.

In movies and in cartoons, I watched the images and heard the messages that the arctic is a desolate place, uncaring, unforgiving, a barren and frozen landscape. I could understand how this view could be true to an outsider. How sad it is, to be so blind to the food and the bounty that is here. I enjoy explaining that the biodiversity in the arctic is tightly packed and presented in miniature versions of a plant's southern relatives. In the same square foot of tundra there can be mosses, lichen, perennial berries and shrubs, forbs, grasses, fungi, spiders, bumblebees, and rodents. How can our homeland be labelled barren when birds migrate thousands of miles to raise their young here?

The view of nature as ungiving and cruel is a Western cultural worldview and although it is arbitrary this view of nature as restrictive and competitive is stated as scientific fact in primary and secondary curriculums. Pre-contact Indigenous population sizes were presented to me in a wide range of guesses—all based on the assumption that North America couldn't possibly support significant populations. Ultimately, every landscape from the arctic to the desert to the forest and the coast are presented in textbooks as unable to care for pre-contact Indigenous populations.

I know in my heart that the land loves humanity, and wants to feed us and wants us to take care of her just as she takes care of us. When the lockdown of the pandemic began, I walked in the forests near my house to relieve stress. I found myself looking closer at the plants with the goal of just knowing where to look because I don't know the traditional foods here as well as I do at home. My efforts would work better if I had an elder to teach and guide me after one of my attempts to gather fiddleheads made me a little nauseous.

Building a good relationship with berries is easier for me and trailing blackberries, one of my favorite PNW native berries, has eluded me for the last twenty years. I knew how delicious and special they are but I would struggle to find enough to store for the winter. The summer of 2020 was the first time that I found a beautiful patch of trailing blackberries, one that was large enough to share with my brother. We wore masks and then happily picked along the patch. My mother was happy for us but she also wished she could have flown down from Alaska and picked with us. Every two to three days I would return to the berry patch and the gift of such special berries was a bright spot during a troubling year.

Although the pandemic kept me from bringing my children to our homeland, I feel a little closer to the plants here. I found a row of tall camas plants growing along both sides of a suburban street and I would walk to them as often as possible while they bloomed and watched for bumblebees visiting. It's a little hard to tell if the camas are wild or planted but it feels good to see them. I fell even deeper in love with the red flowering currant this year and looked for their blooms during my walks. I also learned that my daughter prefers to pick Alaskan berries because they are tastier and visiting our family makes the berry picking trips more fun. I wouldn't have known how my daughter felt about home without the pandemic.

I feel blessed to know what food sovereignty means—a deep and true connection to the land—gathering your own food, touching plants, knowing the conditions of the landscape and the weather patterns, thanking plants and animals, bringing home the food and processing it for storage, and sharing the gifts with your family. I am happy to say that I only know what food sovereignty means in the context of a gift economy. All of these steps for accepting nature's gifts are missing when we simply buy food from the store, there is a physical and emotional distance between us and the land and between us and our families. Food gardening closes this distance some but nothing compares to the humility you feel when you are in a free and wild place and accepting Nature's gifts directly.

Nature wants to take care of all of us and when we accept nature's gifts, we need to remember to do it in a way that respects the ancient relationships to homelands that Indigenous people have maintained since time immemorial. Some Indignous plant foods and medicines are threatened by overharvesting and there are no easy rules for how non-Indigenous peoples can learn to harvest correctly. It's time to let Indigenous people lead the way towards food sovereignty and I feel protective of our knowledge systems. Our ways of taking care of the land are complex and beautiful and our knowledge is something I've never taken for granted, even when I was a little girl learning how to gather herbs for my mother.

Demarus Tevuk (she/her)

Demarus is an Inupiaq from Nome, Alaska and her childhood with Indigenous communities across North America greatly influenced her research on the definition of sustainability from the Indigenous perspective. Demarus earned her degree in Environmental Studies from the University of Washington and she works as an Engagement Strategist with Sustainable Seattle. Demarus loves to pick berries and gather traditional food and she is an avid fiber artist.

RECIPES
& MORE

RECIPE FOR MEMELAS

FORGIVE ME IF THIS RECIPE WAXES A BIT POETIC, BUT I DO HOPE YOU STILL READ AND INDULGE IN IT

- Grab one of those steel mixing bowls you keep in the cabinet.
  - Do you have one of those steel mixing bowl sets that are kind of like russian dolls and have smaller and smaller ones that fit in it? If you do, grab the smallest one. If you don't—if your steel mixing bowl was a hand-me-down that no longer has its brothers and sisters, which were scattered across a grandmother or mother's children so that they all had pieces of her—that is ok, too; grab a small tupperware. This will serve as where you hold lukewarm water. Tiene que estar tibiesita. Don't ask me the science behind it, for I do not know as much. But I know this: the memelas hold better when the water is not frigid.

  - Open the white bag of masa harina.
    - Shake some of that powdered softness (also known as flour) into your large bowl. Maybe give it 3 or 4 shakes.

  - Time to use two hands, or the assistance of a loved one's; with one hand, take the small bowl/tupperware and slowly pour in water; with the other, start to mix the masa.

- Pour in little by little, be sure to refill the water bowl so that it's ready to keep going. Mix the masa with the water. Allow little rivers to form in the harina and then cover them as you fold the slowly-forming-dough into itself.

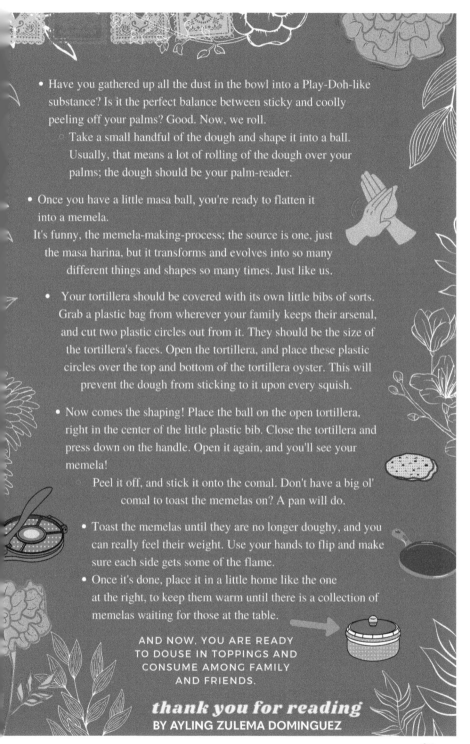

- Have you gathered up all the dust in the bowl into a Play-Doh-like substance? Is it the perfect balance between sticky and coolly peeling off your palms? Good. Now, we roll.
    - Take a small handful of the dough and shape it into a ball. Usually, that means a lot of rolling of the dough over your palms; the dough should be your palm-reader.

- Once you have a little masa ball, you're ready to flatten it into a memela.

It's funny, the memela-making-process; the source is one, just the masa harina, but it transforms and evolves into so many different things and shapes so many times. Just like us.

- Your tortillera should be covered with its own little bibs of sorts. Grab a plastic bag from wherever your family keeps their arsenal, and cut two plastic circles out from it. They should be the size of the tortillera's faces. Open the tortillera, and place these plastic circles over the top and bottom of the tortillera oyster. This will prevent the dough from sticking to it upon every squish.

- Now comes the shaping! Place the ball on the open tortillera, right in the center of the little plastic bib. Close the tortillera and press down on the handle. Open it again, and you'll see your memela!
    - Peel it off, and stick it onto the comal. Don't have a big ol' comal to toast the memelas on? A pan will do.

- Toast the memelas until they are no longer doughy, and you can really feel their weight. Use your hands to flip and make sure each side gets some of the flame.
- Once it's done, place it in a little home like the one at the right, to keep them warm until there is a collection of memelas waiting for those at the table.

AND NOW, YOU ARE READY
TO DOUSE IN TOPPINGS AND
CONSUME AMONG FAMILY
AND FRIENDS.

thank you for reading
BY AYLING ZULEMA DOMINGUEZ

97

Sambar Sadam: You Won't Find This at Your Local Indian Restaurant

By Akhila Sriram

Every culture has a recipe for a warm and comforting soup or stew dish, from congee, to borscht, to chicken noodle soup, to pho. Sambar sadam, also known as bisibelebath, is a South Indian version of that warm stew comfort: a base of lentils and rice, cooked with plenty of spices and veggies, that's always gluten-free and can be vegan if you use oil instead of ghee.

To make this dish, you'll need an InstantPot and you'll need some specific Indian ingredients, including sambar powder. You can get it at any Indian grocery store or on the internet, or even make your own following a recipe from the internet, if you're feeling very ambitious.

These are the instructions my mom told me, which don't do ingredients first/steps second, but mixes steps and measurements together, so read through it first and then figure out what you need, like I did. She also had to force herself to exactly measure out what I needed for the recipe, because I don't have her instincts learned over decades of mastering these dishes. She usually measures out spices in her palm and chucks them into her cooking, which does not work for me, mostly because we have different sized hands. Also disclaimer that she was adapting what sambar sadam usually consists of to what she knew I had in my kitchen, so other recipes out there are probably more accurate, while this one is simplified.

99

1. Put **¼ cup toor daal (yellow lentils)** and **¾ cup rice** into a bowl and cover with water. Use your fingers to swish the daal and rice around in the water to clean off any dust or other particles and slowly drain the cloudy water. Do this 1-2 times more, until the water is less cloudy. Set aside.

2. Chop **one medium onion** (any color), **one bell pepper** (any color), **one potato** (preferably Russet), **one medium zucchini** and **two Roma/small tomatoes**.[1]

3. Turn on the sauté setting on the InstantPot and heat **2 tablespoons of vegetable/canola oil** (or ghee if you have it) in the pot.

4. Once the oil is hot, add **a teaspoon of black mustard seeds**, and back away quickly because you're scared of the seeds' spluttering.

5. Toss in the onion and stir until onion is softened. Then add the bell pepper and stir until that starts to get soft.

6. Turn off the sauté mode and toss in the rest of the veggies and the rinsed rice and daal.

7. In **a cup of hot water**, dissolve **2 tablespoons of sambar powder**.[2] Also toss in **a teaspoon of turmeric** before you forget it. [3]

---

[1]These are the vegetables I had at the time, but you can use other veggies such as green beans, shallots, carrots, turnips, various Asian gourds, or eggplant. Just make sure you have about 3-4 cups of veggies and everything is cut bite-sized.

[2]Except if you look in your cupboard and pull out what you thought was sambar powder, and it turns out to be puliogare powder. In that case, use rasam powder, which is for a different Indian stew, but is close to sambar powder in its spice mix.

[3]Sometimes I forget turmeric accidentally but sometimes on purpose because I think turmeric tastes like dirt, but it has so many good health properties that my mom encourages me to incorporate it in as much of my cooking as possible. It still tastes like dirt.

8. Add this water-spice mixture and **three more cups of water** as well as **2 teaspoons of salt**.

9. Mix everything thoroughly and close the InstantPot, set it to the rice setting, or manual mode for 10 minutes at low pressure.

10. Once it's done, safely quick-release the steam and open up the pot. Assess whether your creation looks more like a soup or a porridge. If soup, leave the lid off so more moisture escapes via steam. You have achieved sambar sadam once it's in a porridge state.

11. *Optional:* Text a picture to the family group chat for validation and bask in the glow of approval of your basic cooking accomplishments from your patti, chittis, and chittappas.

Akhila Sriram (she/her)

Akhila developed a passion for social justice while serving with City Year Seattle King County. She loves reading, binging TV shows and movies, and fangirling over most everything. She works as a technical editor for a market research company and is slowly finishing classes towards her Master's in Library Sciences from the University of Washington.

Vegetarian Lumpia

By Desiree Gabriel

In 2015, I decided to go vegetarian and since then, I have developed my passion for food. But in the last year, my passion for food shifted towards the relational aspects of what nourishes us. In 2020, we all witnessed as the world grappled with COVID-19, which allowed many of us to value community initiatives far more than before. I also watched as the world stood up to systemic and covert racism, especially against people within the Black, Indigenous, and Asian communities. I watched as numerous family-owned restaurants shut down during the pandemic, like those in Chinatowns around North America. My friends and I were pushed to unpack our own internalized biases and racism. I was led back into Asian cuisine. I mean, I had the time for it now under lockdown, right? The pandemic forced me along the path of reclaiming my traditional foods (vegetarianized), with numerous ups and downs in the kitchen.

If you know anything about traditional Filipino food, you know that it's meat intensive. Because of that, I have barely eaten Filipino food in the past 6 years of being vegetarian, and most of the recipes I have cooked were "Western" styled cuisine. So when I made vegan lumpia to end off 2020, my heart was more full than my stomach. Since our lives have shifted largely towards a digital domain, I looked to content creators for inspiration. I followed BIPOC plant-based Instagrammers like @chez_jorge, @thecanadianafrican, and @the.korean.vegan in order to learn more about diverse cultural foods that I could eat as a vegetarian. I also found accounts that lit something in my heart. @godofcookery, @sophia_roe, and @chinatownfoundation enable an online and accessible learning experience based on respectability politics in the food industry. I have definitely grown due to these people in understanding the sacredness of cultural foods. I urge you to do the same.

With Luv,
Desiree

103

Makes 30 pieces

Filling

1 medium sized carrot, grated

½ white onion, diced

4 garlic cloves, minced

8 dried shiitake mushrooms, rehydrated and diced

340 g meat alternative (I used Impossible: Burger Made from Plants)

salt and pepper to taste

optional: ¾ of an egg

Wraps + "glue"

½ pack of spring roll sheets cut into quarters (if you are vegan, double check these do not contain egg, as many do!)

1 tbsp cornstarch or flour

100 mL of warm water

Optional: ¼ of an egg instead of the cornstarch or flour slurry

For frying

¼ inch layer of vegetable oil in skillet

Instructions

1. Mix all of the filling ingredients in a medium sized bowl. Add salt and pepper to taste, and feel free to add more or less of any of the ingredients, based on your preferences. Lumpia is fun because you can freestyle it to match your preferences! If you are not vegan, adding ¾ egg allows the ingredients to stick together more coherently.

2. In a ramekin, whisk cornstarch or flour into warm water. This will act as 'glue' for your spring roll sheets. Using ¼ egg is more secure, but if you are vegan then cornstarch and water will work just fine.

3. Place a quartered spring roll sheet onto a flat surface (I used a plate) ensuring it is in the shape of a diamond, and not squared. Add about ½ a heaping tbsp of filling, in the shape of a log, onto the middle of your sheet. The filling should be horizontal. You're going to fold the right and left corners in,

and place them on top of the filling. Pull the bottom corner up. Do this with love and care, you don't want to break the wrapper!

4. Use your finger to glide the 'glue' onto the top corner of the sheet, and roll the lumpia so it sits on top of the glue.

5. Repeat for the next ~30 rolls. Don't worry, you will get better and faster as you practice (assemble a small pandemic-responsible team to make this process more enjoyable).

6. Pour ~1/4 inch of oil in a skillet on medium heat. After about 4 minutes, you can test the oil by placing a chopstick in it; if the chopsticks bubble then you're ready to go!

7. Place lumpia, sealed-side down, into the skillet, ensuring they are not touching. Wait about 2 minutes, or until they are golden brown, and flip them with chopsticks or a set of tongs. Do the same on the other side and place them onto paper towels placed over a tray. The paper towels will absorb excess oil.

8. Serve with your choice of spicy banana ketchup, sweet and sour sauce, or good old ketchup.

P.S. I hope you enjoy the lumpia as much as I did! Lumpia represents celebrations, gatherings, and community. Since most Filipinos know how to make them, you can always find them at our functions. My favourite thing about lumpia is that you can alter the ratio of ingredients depending on what you and your family likes!

Desiree Gabriel (she/her)
Desiree is a Filipina-Canadian pescatarian. She studies environmental geography and urban studies at UBC, and spends the free time she can muster by cooking (obviously), playing piano, snowboarding, reading, sketching, and watching anime. She is currently learning ASL and Japanese, and relearning French and Tagalog. If you are also practicing these languages feel free to message her to become language learning buddies! Instagram: @desireegabriel

Aromatic SLEE Salmon

By Heather Day and Travis English

CAGJ has traditionally served salmon at our annual Strengthening Local Economies Everywhere (SLEE) dinner thanks to the generosity of Loki Fish Co., who have donated 30 whole salmon to every SLEE dinner for the past 15 years. We weren't able to gather in person in 2020, but still managed to distribute Loki salmon to our Table Captains and Solidarity Campaign partners so we could all enjoy a salmon meal at home during our virtual event!

Ingredients

1 whole wild salmon

½ fennel bulb, sliced

½ red onion, sliced

3 garlic cloves, chopped

1 orange, any variety, sliced

1 TBSP sweet smoked paprika

Instructions

1. Toss above ingredients with cooking oil, salt and pepper.

2. Rub inside and outside of whole salmon with mixture of cooking oil, salt and pepper.

3. Stuff salmon with above ingredients; if any are left over, roast them in pan with salmon.

4. Bake at 425°F until internal temperature is 140 degrees, 30-60 minutes depending on the size of the salmon.

5. Remove salmon and increase oven temperature to broil.

6. Broil to crisp salmon skin, until internal temperature reaches 160°F, 5-10 minutes.

To watch this recipe being prepared...

Visit the digital zine:
https://zine.cagj.org/recipes/heather-travis/

Heather Day (she/her) & **Travis English** (he/him)
Heather Day helped to found CAGJ after the 1999 WTO protests, and has loved acting as CAGJ's Director since 2007. Travis English is Heather's husband and co-conspirator. They co-created the idea of SLEE—CAGJ's annual community celebration—while on a road trip to Baja, Mexico. Travis has been the SLEE chef most years, and was a well-known fixture of the Ballard Farmers Market pre-Covid. They enjoy raising their son Henry in West Seattle where they're cultivating community and turning their lawn into a veggie and flower garden.

Finding my way home

following the scent of cedar
upriver

spawning salmon
in the heart of my child

—MORGAN BROWN, "TASTING THE STARS"

Grilled Sourdough Tartine

with grilled carrots and kale pesto, pickled beets and chèvre

By Benjamin Jones

I love this recipe because it is earthy, homey, healthy, inexpensive and unpretentious. It is one that will always impress folks but isn't too complicated. This is also a recipe that can be really easily altered with the seasons. This is one that I always return to in my menus. During the winter, carrots, beets and kale are great but during the summer you can get really creative with it. I often add mushrooms to this recipe, a favorite food of mine. Mushrooms are so versatile and packed with nutrients. They are perfect for someone who is looking for ways to move away from a classic American meat filled diet; they can be manipulated in so many ways and can be substituted for a dish that calls for meat. Mushrooms are the great communicators of the natural world and are a food I hold a lot of respect for.

I love to cook because I love the surprises food can hold. Seeing the joy you can bring to a room when you cook something that is interesting and fun and engaging and in tune with the land around you is so satisfying. I also love a good challenge and there is always more to learn in the world of food and cooking, there is never a point where you are done studying and growing and learning as a chef, which makes this work so much more motivating for me. Right now, I am working as the sous chef at a spot called Bis on Main in Bellevue. If you are in the area, come on in and ask for me, I would love to hear your experience with this recipe! I hope you enjoy this recipe and don't forget to get creative with it and use what you have access to in order to make this delicious and perfect for you.

Ingredients

Local bakery sourdough cut into approx. 2" slices

4 medium rainbow carrots

2-3 golden beets

3 cups Lacinato kale

2 oz package of goat chèvre
(such as Laura Chenel)

4 oz extra virgin olive oil

Juice from 1 lemon

4 cloves garlic

1 cup red wine vinegar

Salt and pepper to taste

Instructions

1. Preheat oven to 375°F.

2. Poke holes in beets with a fork and toss them in olive oil and salt. Place on baking tray and put in oven for around 25 minutes until tender but not soft.

3. With a towel, peel beets and slice into thin strips.

4. In a 1qt sauce pot bring vinegar and 2 cloves smashed garlic to a boil. Add beets, turn off heat and leave to rest.

5. De-stem kale and place in large mixing bowl. Add 2 cloves diced garlic, olive oil, lemon juice and a pinch of salt. Massage until tender. Transfer to food processor and blend until smooth and season with salt and pepper to taste.

6. On a grill, season carrots with olive oil, salt and pepper. Char on outside until soft in middle, around 5 minutes. Can also use cast iron skillet for 3 minutes and broil for 3 minutes.

7. Grill bread on both sides until warm and slightly charred. Again, can use cast iron skillet. Brush with olive oil.

8. Spread chèvre on grilled bread, add carrots and top with pesto and pickled beets.

Benjamin Jones (he/him)

I am a Muscogee and Black chef located on occupied Duwamish land. I am passionate about sharing stories through food and finding creative ways to make sustainable, healthy food also taste bomb. I love to learn new techniques and ways to honor the food we have been blessed with. On my days off, I am happiest when I am on a hike with my partner and our dog!

Flor de Calabaza

Por Evelin Alvarado

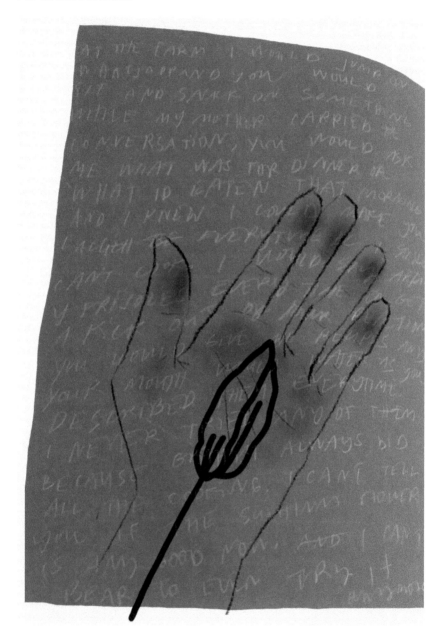

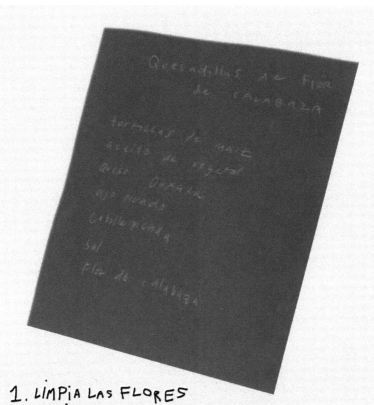

1. LIMPIA LAS FLORES
2. CALIENTA EL ACEITE Y AGREGA LA CEBOLLA, EL AJO, Y LAS FLORES
3. SAZONA CON SAL Y PIMIENTA
4. COLOCA EL QUESITO EN UNA TORTILLA SOBRE EL COMAL
5. AÑADE EL GUISADO DE FLOR

Ingredientes

tortillas de maíz	cebolla picada
aceite de vegetal	sal
queso Oaxaca	flor de calabaza
ajo picado	

Instrucciones

1. Limpia las flores

2. Calienta el aceite y agrega la cebolla, el ajo, y las flores

3. Sazona con sal y pimienta

4. Coloca el quesito en una tortilla sobre el comal

5. Añade el guisado de flor

Evelin Alvarado (she/her)
Evelin is a senior studying social work at the University of Oklahoma. She is undocumented and an advocate for immigrant rights, community healing, and transformative justice. Evelin is passionate about creating space and sharing art, and uses crafting and reading as a way to resist, connect, and heal with those she loves.

Aunque nuestros jardines parezcan difíciles de crear o mantener, aunque en un principio no sepamos qué hacer, aunque muchos los destruyan, accidentalmente o intencionalmente, siempre habrá valido la pena sembrar una semilla.

—DELIA PINTO-SANTINI, "JARDINES DE PANDEMIA"

Roasted Root Vegetable Soup

By Laura Titzer

Ingredients

honestly, any root veggies will do!

¼ cup olive oil

3-4 sweet potatoes, cut into chunks

2 carrots, cut into thick rounds

1 celeriac, cut into chunks

8 oz white beans (these could be canned if in a pinch, otherwise, Vermont cranberry or Calypso from local farmers are great)

1 onion, quartered

3 bay leaves

Thyme sprigs, or about a ½ teaspoon dried

Rosemary sprigs, or about a ½ teaspoon dried

5 cups vegetable stock

Salt and pepper

Instructions

1. Preheat oven to 400°F.

2. Toss all the veggies with the oil and then spread out on a baking sheet. Try to do a single layer if you have multiple baking sheets. If not, make sure to turn them more frequently.

3. Tuck the bay leaves, thyme, and rosemary among the veggies.

4. Roast for 50 minutes or until tender. Turn the vegetables to try and get them to brown on as many sides as possible.

5. Once removed from the oven, discard the bay leaves and sprigs (if using) and transfer the vegetables to a large saucepan.

6. Pour the stock into the pan and bring to a boil. Reduce heat, and simmer for about 10 minutes. Next, either use a hand blender/immersion blender or food processor/blender and process until thick and smooth.

7. Return soup to pan and add salt and pepper as desired. Ready!

Chicken Tortilla Soup

By Evelyn Costello

2 TBSP oil

1 white onion

2 jalapeños, finely diced
(discard seeds if you don't
want it as spicy)

3-4 cloves of minced garlic

**6 cups of good quality
chicken broth**

**14.5 oz can of fire roasted
diced tomatoes**

**14.5 oz can of rinsed black
beans**

3 boneless chicken breasts

2 limes

**1 cup roughly chopped
cilantro**

Salt and Pepper

Cumin

Chili

3 bay leaves

Toppings

Sliced avocado

Tortilla strips

Monterey Jack cheese

Instructions

1. Heat oil in a large pot over medium heat. Add onions and cook till soft (about 2 minutes).

2. Add your garlic and jalapeños and cook for another minute.

3. Add broth, tomatoes, beans, cumin, chili, bay leaves, and bring to a boil. Salt and pepper to taste.

4. Lower to a simmer and add the chicken breasts.

5. Cook for 20-25 minutes and remove the chicken once cooked. Let cool and shred.

6. Add your shredded chicken to a bowl and ladle your soup over it. Top with avocado, cheese, and tortilla strips.

Southwest Salad with Vegan Chili Dressing

By Kirsten Spooner

Makes 5 Servings

Salad Ingredients

½ head of romaine

1 cup of kale, chopped

1 medium bell pepper

1 medium tomato

1 large avocado, chopped

½ cup red onion, diced

2 scallions

¼ cup cilantro, minced

1 can black beans (15 oz cooked beans)

1 ear corn or 1 can corn (15 oz)

½ jalapeño, diced (optional)

Corn tortilla chips for topping

Dressing

½ cup veganaise

¼ cup sriracha (or to taste)

Juice of 1 lime

Instructions

1. Roast corn in a nonstick skillet with diced jalapeno until the corn begins to brown (around 5 mins).

2. While corn is roasting, start chopping and dicing your veggies.

3. Prepare dressing by whisking all ingredients together in a bowl.

4. In a large salad bowl add all the veggies and beans, topping with roasted corn and jalapeño mixture.

5. Toss with dressing.

Notes

If you are storing some salad to eat throughout the week, toss dry ingredients together and keep dressing, tortilla strips and avocado on the side until you are serving. Once sliced, avocado will not last more than a day or so away from the pit and dressing makes everything soggy!

Pickled Onions

By Maegan McCoy

Ingredients

Thinly sliced large red onion

1 cup water

½ cup white vinegar

½ cup rice vinegar and/or red wine vinegar

3 TBSP maple syrup or honey

1.5 TBSP salt

Instructions

1. Boil brine then pour over onions in container. When room temperature place in fridge. Use when brine turns pink.

2. The excess onion skins can be boiled to make a light pink dye.

> **See Maegan's cornhusk dolls dyed with onion skins on page 58!**

Maegan McCoy (she/her)

Hello, I am a queer multimedia artist, currently studying Cinema and Art at the UO. I have more time to cook for myself now that I have a kitchen in my apartment and classes are remote. Recently, I've become obsessed with fermentation. I have two sourdough starters and multiple bottles of homemade kombucha in the fridge as we speak. I've always longed for a closer relationship to what I eat and have a strong passion for cooking and food sovereignty. Visit my website at https://maeganmccoyart.com.

Joyce's Meat Sauce Bolognese

By Grace Miyoshi

Ingredients

6 tomato cans (14 oz; the average canned-beans, canned-vegetable size)

1.5 lbs ground pork (can do half beef, or meat substitute for vegetarians)

3 cloves garlic

1 onion

3 carrots

3 ribs celery (as many leafy parts as possible)

3 bay leaves (or sage)

3 bouillon cubes (chicken, beef, or vegetable)

400 cc (about 1¾ cup) red wine, room temperature

Salt/pepper

Olive oil

Instructions

1. Prepare veggies:
- Chop the carrots, onion, and celery finely (can use a food processor). Mince the garlic.
- Place 3-4 tablespoons of olive oil in pan and add garlic.
- Simmer garlic slowly over medium heat. Do not burn!
- Once garlic flavor transfers to oil, add the rest of the veggies. Add salt and pepper.
- Simmer veggies until reduced to about 3 quarters.

2. Prepare meat:
- Add meat into the heated pot and add salt and pepper.
- Simmer meat until meat edges become crispy (meat liquid needs to be absorbed back in).
- Add red wine in the pot (make sure the pot is hot and the wine's liquid flies off).
- Simmer until meat absorbs the wine and there is no liquid left.

3. Add meat, veggies and tomatoes:
- Add all together and raise heat until it boils (adjust the number of tomato cans based on how meaty you want it).
- Add in sage leaves, bouillon, salt and pepper.
- Lower heat to mid-low heat once it boils.
- Simmer until flavor settles (30-60 minutes).

Joyce's Japanese Mince Meat Curry

By Grace Miyoshi

Ingredients

800 grams ground pork

2 onions, diced

4 large carrots

5 stems of celery + leafy parts

4 chicken soup cubes

1 pack of curry paste cubes (Japanese store e.g. Golden Curry)

1 tablespoon nutmeg

1 tablespoon cardamom

6 cloves garlic

7 chili peppers (or red chili flakes to taste)

4 oregano leaves

2 (14 ounce) can chickpeas, rinsed and drained

1 bunch fresh parsley, chopped

1 cup red wine

3 tablespoons cooking oil

3 cups water

salt and pepper (to taste)

Instructions

1. Chop garlic (keep separate), onions, carrots, and celery. Use food processors to speed up the process.

2. Warm the pot with cooking oil with garlic slowly to let the flavor out. Then add chopped vegetables. Let them sweat until volume is reduced about 25%. Put aside.

3. Heat up same pot again and cook minced pork. Patiently cook until all liquids are evaporated and flavor goes back into pork. This takes a while.

4. When the pot sizzles with the edges of pork a bit crispy, add in the wine and stir until all wine is evaporated.

5. Mix back in the vegetables, add water, chickpeas, soup cubes, chili pepper, oregano leaves and let simmer for 10 minutes.

6. Add in curry cubes & adjust to taste with salt, pepper, nutmeg and cardamom. Add water to adjust to your preferred consistency.

7. Serve with rice or bread. Can also freeze and save for later, or make into pies—yumm!! Can definitely halve the portions to make less, but in this curry's case, more tends to be better.

For more about Grace's recipes, see "A Soffritto Story" on page 24.

Sourdough Crackers

By Hillary Haden

Ingredients

1 cup flour

1 cup sourdough starter, unfed

½ tsp salt

4 TBSP butter

2 TBSP herbs (I like oregano, but rosemary or any herb of your choice will work!)

Oil to brush on top

Instructions

1. Mix ingredients.

2. Cover and let sit for 30 minutes or until the dough is firm.

3. Roll the dough out on a floured piece of wax or parchment paper until the dough is 1/16 of an inch thick.

4. Brush with oil and cut into smaller cracker-sized squares.

5. Bake at 350°F for 20-25 minutes.

6. Enjoy with cream cheese, marinara, hummus, a little peanut butter, or another topping of your choice.

Read Hillary's piece "A Recipe for a Resilient Global Economy" on page 53!

Nettle & Lemon Balm Tea

By David Rollins

Instructions

1. Take a walk to your nearest wooded riparian area during mid spring, while keeping an eye out for tall growing nettle plants. Bring along shears and a thick pair of work gloves. These will look a bit like large mint plants, with hairy stems. You'll know it's nettle when these hairs bring a sharp sting to the back of your hand.

2. With a proper ID, harvest the broad leaves. Trim in a way that leaves the upper most leaves intact, especially at the points of growth so that this nettle grove will stay healthy for generations to come while remembering Robin Wall Kimmerer's advice, "never take more than half."

3. Bring these leaves home for dehydrating.

---

4. On another walk in a bit higher elevation, or if you are lucky in the same outing, keep your eye out for wild lemon balm. Lemon balm will also look like mint, this time about the same size but with a sharp lemon smell when pinched between the fingers.

5. Repeat steps 2-3 with the lemon balm (except that lemon balm is non-endemic, so it's okay to take a bit more than half. This is citizen-conservation).

---

6. With dehydrated leaves of both at home, boil a kettle of water.

7. Add two-parts nettle to one-part lemon balm to loose-leaf tea steeper. For one cup of tea, make this: two teaspoons of nettle to one teaspoon of lemon balm.

8. Let steep for ten to twelve minutes.

9. Remove tea leaves. Add honey to taste.

Enjoy, knowing you've foraged from the natural world and took part in a bit of non-endemic species control.

Black Pepper Onions

By Tess Keesling

Makes 1 Quart

Ingredients & Equipment

900 grams sliced onions

20 grams coarse unrefined sea salt

15 grams whole black peppercorns

50 milliliters natural brine from a basic kraut (this can be from a store bought kraut or one you've maybe already made)

Kitchen scale

1-quart wide mouth mason jar

Weight

Fermentation lid

Check out Tess's art on page 22!

Instructions

1. Wash and sanitize all your fermentation equipment, including a medium bowl, knife, and cutting board, and set aside to air dry.

2. In the medium bowl, combine the onions, salt, peppercorns, and kraut brine. With clean (or gloved) hands, massage, squeeze, and mix the onions until they begin to release liquid, about 2 minutes. When you can grab a handful of onions and squeeze the liquid out of it easily, it's ready to go.

3. Transfer the onions to the jar along with any liquid. As you add the onions tamp them down with your fist to submerge the solids under the brine and force out any air pockets. Continue until the jar is almost full, leaving 1 to 2 inches of headspace.

4. Place the weight in the jar on top of the onions and press down until the onions are completely submerged in brine. Seal the jar with the fermentation lid. Place the sealed jar in a bowl to catch any liquid displaced through the airlock during fermentation.

5. Ferment the onions in a cool place away from direct sunlight (3 weeks at 64°F is ideal). Taste the onions after 2 weeks to determine if the flavor and sourness are to your liking. If they're not sour enough, reseal the jar and let them ferment for another week, then taste again. When the onions taste good, replace the fermentation lid with a regular lid, seal, and store in the refrigerator for up to 10 months.

Sweet Beans

By Zain Alsharari

My mom used to make a meal of sweet beans for us, and we would have it with Arabic bread. During the quarantine, I thought about making it. Since I didn't have the Arabic bread and it was a difficult time to get out for unnecessary stuff, I thought about eating it with white rice. I cooked the rice with only cloves and cardamom, which made it very tasty.

Ingredients

onions

olive oil

1 can white beans

tomato sauce

1 small spoon sugar

Instructions

1. Fry onions in olive oil until they become slightly brown.

2. Add white beans, tomato sauce, sugar.

3. Let it cook for 5-10 minutes.

Notes

You can replace the tomato sauce and the sugar with just ketchup.

Zain Alsharari

My family called me Zain and it's pronounced Zain as you pronounce Rain. My native language is Arabic. My favorite way to eat potatoes is to eat it with my home-town's olive oil.

Vegan Almond Cookies

By Na Haby Stella Faye

I am passionate about food. Maybe because I'm Italian. And a Taurus.

Food has been all my life a great vehicle for emotions and values. This is the reason why in 2020 I chose to volunteer at an organic farm on the gentle hills of Marostica, Italy and follow some cooking courses; to reconnect with myself and the earth after a rollercoaster of a year through clean, healthy and fair nutrition and food production.

Permaculture teaches you to observe and listen to what nature suggests, and this is what I did during the month I spent there. I would work on fruit trees or in the vegetable garden, learning about silence and care. And then stop every couple hours, to breathe the sun, the cold air, the smell of weeds, to remember to listen.

When it was raining, and the soil was too damp to be worked on, I would bake in the warmth of a soft coloured kitchen. I had the opportunity to participate in a vegan pastry-making class from the "Centro di Alimentazione Consapevole" (Conscious Nutrition Centre, Naples, Italy), where I learned the cookie recipe I am sharing with you. Baking and learning about the amazing, healing power of food was a cathartic experience for the whole of me, mind, body and feelings. I hope this recipe can instill some of this light in all of you!

Ingredients

160 grams (1½ cup) whole wheat flour

40 grams (⅓ cup) almonds (finely chopped)

70 grams (⅓ cup) raw cane sugar (if you are avoiding sugar you can substitute with the same amount of finely chopped dry fruit, such as raisins, figs, dates etc.)

40 grams (⅕ cup) seed oil (I usually use sunflower seed or corn germ oil)

90 mL (⅓ cup) apple juice (if using dry fruits instead of sugar you might need less)

Instructions

1. Preheat the oven at 350°F (180°C).

2. Mix the flour, almonds and sugar in a large bowl. If you are using raisins instead of sugar, rehydrate them in a bowl with water, chop them with a chopper or food processor and add them to the other dry ingredients.

3. Add the oil, mix and gradually pour the apple juice, in case less than 90 mL is needed.

4. When the dough is smooth and homogeneous, use a rolling pin to roll it out and use stamps to form the cookies.

5. Put the cookies in the oven for 12 minutes. Take them out when the dough is still slightly soft, as they will harden once out of the oven.

6. Let your cookies cool for at least half an hour, enjoy! :)

Na Haby Stella Faye (she/her)

I am a Senegalese-Italian nature lover! I have a bachelor's degree in international relations and I recently approached the world of sustainable food systems, hoping to contribute to the just transition to a socially, economically and environmentally sustainable future!

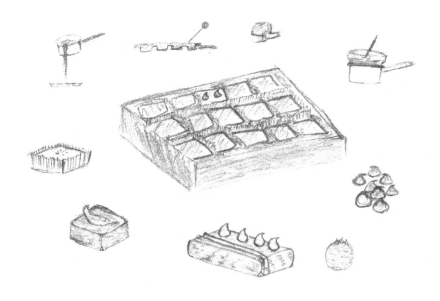

Vegan Chocolate Truffles

Recipe by Cora Boynton; Drawing by Desmond Boynton

During quarantine, it is really easy to feel like every day is the same. One of the best ways to cope with boredom for me has always (and especially now) been spending time in the kitchen. These delicious vegan chocolate truffles are perfect as gifts to brighten up boring days for other people or to treat yourself. They work really well for storing (1-2 months in the freezer or a week in the fridge). They are rich, sweet, and chocolaty, and it is easy to experiment and invent lots of new flavors.

Makes About 30 Truffles

½ cup coconut milk (or your milk of choice)

2 TBSP coconut oil

1 cup (6 oz or 175 grams) dark chocolate chips (Fair Trade if you can!)

Instructions

1. Combine coconut milk and coconut oil in a small saucepan and heat on medium until boiling.

2. Remove from heat, take chocolate chips and pour them into the milk/oil mixture. Swirl the mixture over the chocolate so that it is covered fully in milk, but don't mix. Cover the pan and let sit for 5 minutes undisturbed.

3. Take the lid off and mix melted chocolate and milk together with a spatula until smooth and glossy. If you want, add any flavorings from our list or your imagination to the ganache right now. Put ganache in the fridge to harden for about 30-45 minutes or until firm enough to roll.

Flavors to add:
Peppermint
Lemon, orange, or lime zest
Raspberry
Strawberry
Fennel
Curry powder
Coriander
Cardamom
Cinnamon
Rosewater
Chipotle powder
Pomegranate molasses

4. Once the ganache is firm, take it out of the fridge. Take a small ball of the ganache onto your hands and roll it into a ball, repeating with the rest of your chocolate.

5. Take your truffles and roll them in prepared ingredients. We recommend cocoa powder, coconut flakes or toasted coconut flakes, toasted sesame seeds, chopped roasted nuts, chopped chocolate, or cacao nibs, but you can use any related things too.

6. Place in the fridge to firm up a little bit before serving.

7. Enjoy!!!

If you want to, you could also dip in melted or tempered chocolate and garnish with:

Fancy or flavored salt or sugar
Mint leaves
Rose petals
Chile powders
Ground spices

Cora (she/her) and **Desmond** (he/him) **Boynton**

Cora Boynton, age 13, loves making vegan baked goods, truffles, and caramels. Her brother Desmond, age 11, helps come up with designs and garnishes for her creations. Someday, they hope to open a vegan chocolate shop together. You can follow Cora's blog at yummyveganbakes.com.

For a printable version of this fortune teller...

Visit the digital zine:
https://zine.cagj.org/art/sam-erika/

ENVISIONING FUTURES WITH FORTUNE TELLERS!
BY SAM & ERIKA

In the spirit of this larger zine project and "reflecting on the future" as we moved into 2021, we wanted to work together to collectively engage with the questions of "What do you envision for the future? How do we get there?" With this practice and workshop we'd collaborate to gather ideas, and each emerge with our own paper fortuneteller to help us map the futures we are working towards. We'd navigate a "new normal" together. So often the idea of the future can be overwhelming, creating fortunetellers is a joyful way to look ahead.

For Erika, creating and facilitating this workshop was a way to think about how to engage people in more creative ways and build more relationships in organizing and activism. It was really exciting and interesting to hear the ways that people engaged with the prompts and created their fortune tellers. It was very fufilling to hear folks responses, beyond what Erika could even imagine on her own.

Sam was curious what it would look like to playfully and meaningfully engage with what it means to shape the future. How could we work backwards, together? How could we get present, in whatever emotions we are in right now and PLAY with that to edd us back to some visionary future we so desperately want and need? With these fortune tellers, we state the future as a fact. We are there, we've made it happen! How did we do it? It certainly wasn't neat and easy; but we will have flexed the gifts and overcome the barriers of everything along the way. So let's play! We're manifesting, baby.

Instructions:
Cut or tear across bottom line
Fold square in half diagonally
one-way then the opposite
Folded line should make an X
across center
Fold all corners in to center point
Flip paper so folded points face
down towards work surface
Fold new corners into center
point
Once folded crease along "+"
Crease edges then unfold
creases

To play:
Ask the player to pick an emotion from the top
four of the fortuneteller
Spell out that emotion, sounding it out while you
shuffle the fortuneteller
Have them pick a feeling from the inside of the
fortune teller
Now sound that feeling out while shuffling the
fortune teller again
Have them pick another feeling from inside the
fortune teller
This will reveal the future!

CREATE YOUR OWN FORTUNE TELLER

PROMPTS:

Envision a future you want to see. What are some things that are the "new normal"?

How do you feel now, or *want* to feel about the future?

For each feeling word, consider,
What is a gift of that feeling?
What is a detriment of that feeling?

HOW TO:

Come up with eight.
Write these as statements of fact on inner triangles labeled (A)

eg: PRISONS ARE OBSOLETE, EVERYONE CAN GROW FOOD, ETC...

Begin with a list of four or more feeling words

Choose four to write on panels labeled (B)

eg: JOYFUL, HESITANT, INSPIRED, DISHEARTENED

Write one for each emotion, choosing four gifts and four barriers total
Write one on each panel labeled (C)

eg: HESITANT:
gift: critical thinking
barrier: missed opportunities

Anna Banks

School and work semi-permanently moved into our homes

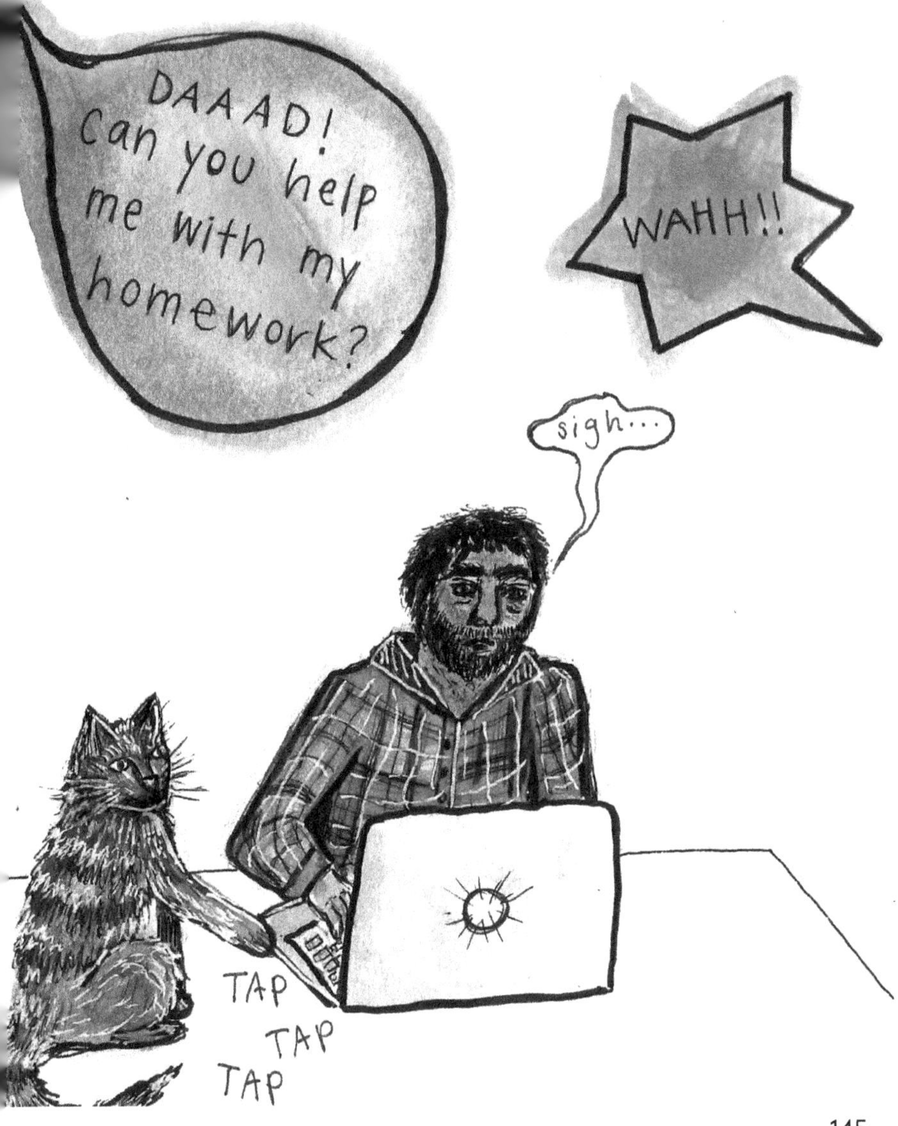

we had to stay away from our
loved ones to keep each other
safe and look out for their
health

and many of the things that we loved to do together as a community shut down

But through all of the grief, the anger, the sadness, the waiting...

149

friends and community

spending time in nature

look Mama!
BIG LEAF

pets and
other small
animal friends

we started learning how
to take care of ourselves

and learned how to care
for each other

The more we slowed our lives, the more we grew into who we were meant to be.

We learned to deconstruct and unlearn harmful things that we were taught:

that's not my problem...

no sleep!

work, work, work

individualism

push your feelings down

self-loathing

power through

grind culture

dressing for the male gaze

don't cry

don't tell anyone what happened

I'm not racist

I don't need help

abelism

overconsumption

generous

selfless

native

empathetic

intuitive

justice-seeking

And began to accept ourselves and each other for who we are

loving

silly

in community

listen to our bodies and feelings

accepting

diverse

rested

growing

queer

If we try to do what is good, selfless, and healin[g] like...

DO SOMETHING SILLY!

THINK OF OTHERS! REST!! MUTUAL VOTE! GO
AID!!

FORGIVE YOURSELF!! SHARE RESOURCES!!

DANCE MORE!

DISMANTLE SYSTEMS OF INJUSTIC[E]

SELF-ACCEPTANCE!! SIGN SOME PETITIONS

SPEND TIME IN NATURE!! WEAR A MAS[K]

LOVE YOUR HOUSELESS NEIGHBOR!! TAKE YOUR MEDS

PET A WEE CAT OR DOG (IF ABLE)

CALL YOUR LOCAL REPRESENT[ATIVE]

FILL YOUR COMMUNITY PANTRY!

CRY

ICE!..
ERAPY!!
STAY HOME.
REDISTRIBUTE WEALTH
COMMUNITY CAR
TELL SOMEONE THAT GIVE TO THOSE
YOU LOVE THEM!! IN NEED!!
OLISH THE PRISON INDUSTRIAL COMPLE
Z! RECONNECT WITH YOUR EAT GOOD FOOD CREA
INNER CHILD!! TOGETHER!
WASH YOUR HANDS!! BREATHE
IP SERVICE WORKERS ALLOW YOURSELF TO LAUGH!
VES! GRIEVE CALL YOUR GRANDMA MORE! CRY IF YOU NEED TO
HUG SOMEONE!!
START A GARDEN! (SAFELY PLZ::)
OLD ABUSERS LOVE YOUR LOCAL
COUNTABLE! HEALTHCARE WORKERS!
REST AGAIN!! SHOP LOCAL!! AFF(IRM SOMEONE THAT
(Because it's NEEDS TO HEAR IT!!
important) STAND UP FOR
YOURSELF!
HEAL

157

then eventually,
when the world is
safer and healthier

we can come back together as people that care for one another

and spread love wherever we are

Anna Banks (she/they)

I'm a Queer, Jewish human from Eugene, Oregon studying environmental science and making art! I am a vertebrate paleontology researcher and am currently writing and illustrating a children's book about mushrooms! I believe that life is meant for appreciating small moments, sensations, good food, and the company of other lovely humans. I hope to use art and writing to further connect with local communities.

カリフォルニア 柿
(California Kaki)

Lara Ruegg (she/her)

I'm Lara, I currently live on Duwamish Land, but I grew up on Wappo Land in California! I grew up with a hachiya persimmon tree in my back yard. I climbed it, fell out of it, and watched birds get tipsy off the rotten fruit in the fall. While we didn't eat the fruit fresh, we would share them with my grandma, who would dry or bake them. Food was always the thing that connected me to my Japanese roots, and this tree was a big part of that connection.

Art by Sam Shafer

THANK YOU!

Zine Organizing Collective

Momo Wilms-Crowe
David Rollins
Pukhraj Sidhu
Nuansi
Alanna Peterson
Heather Day
Delia Pinto-Santini

Sam Shafer
Erika Mazza-Smith
Sara Lavenhar
Sophia Kimble
Connor Nakamura
Noël Hutton
Lynx Patrice Hawthorn

Zine Sponsors

Many thanks to our sponsors: *Central Co-op, Marc Auerbach, Ellysia Banks, Sara Lavenhar, Niaz Dorry, Orion Montoya, and Kristel Peterson.*

Much gratitude also goes out to the many many more grassroots donors who donated to our community-supported publishing campaign, bought tickets in our #PayOurArtists raffle fundraiser, and otherwise contributed!

Zine Contributors

This zine would not exist without the contributions of the amazingly talented artists who shared their creations with us! We are so grateful to you all. Additionally, a special thanks to Morgan Brown for providing this publication's cover art.